REMAKING THE

ARGENTINE

ECONOMY

AXS 0014 - 3/2

REMAKING THE ARGENTINE ECONOMY

Felipe A. M. de la Balze

COUNCIL ON FOREIGN RELATIONS PRESS

NEW YORK

COUNCIL ON FOREIGN RELATIONS BOOKS

Library of Congress Cataloging-in-Publication Data

Balze, Felipe A. M. de la.
    Remaking the Argentine economy / by Felipe A.M. de la Balze.
       p.   cm.
    Includes bibliographical references and index.
    ISBN 0-87609-171-0 : $14.95
    1. Argentina—Economic policy.   2. Argentina—Economic conditions.
  I. Title.
  HC175.B26   1994
  338.982—dc20   94-40865
                                         CIP

95   96   97   98   EB   10   9   8   7   6   5   4   3   2   1

Cover design: Dorothy Wachtenheim

CONTENTS

PREFACE

Sustained economic growth is one of the primary goals of national economic policy, but this has been an elusive goal for Argentina. In this book, I begin with a brief discussion of Argentina's postwar economic and institutional decline, followed by a review of the reforms and profound changes that have occurred during the last few years. I have also, somewhat ambitiously, attempted to single out the key issues that Argentina still needs to face if it wishes to provide a solid and permanent foundation for the political and economic reforms underway.

This book was presented to and reviewed by an American study group that met at the Council on Foreign Relations on several occasions during 1992 and 1993. Simultaneously, an Argentine study group met at the Consejo Argentino de Relaciones Internacionales (CARI). An earlier version of this work was presented at a joint session of both study groups organized by the Council on Foreign Relations in June 1993.

I would like to express my special appreciation to Ambassador Williams H. Luers (Metropolitan Museum of Art), Paul Meo (World Bank), Dr. Martha Muse (Tinker Foundation), and Professor David Rock (University of California, Santa Barbara), whose written comments have helped enrich this book.

On the Argentine side, I am deeply indebted to the president of CARI, Ambassador Carlos Muñiz, for his permanent support and to the members of the CARI study group, who met regularly over the course of a year and provided detailed comments on every aspect of the initial draft: Daniel Artana (FIEL), Jorge C. Avila (CEMA), Enrique A. Bour (Central Bank), Rosendo Fraga (Centro de Estudios Union para la Nueva Mayoría), Javier González Fraga (Instituto Argentino de Mercado de Capitales), Ricardo López Murphy (FIEL), Manuel Mora y Araujo (Estudio Mora Araujo, Noguera y Asociados), and Julio J. Nogues (World Bank). I wish to thank Norberto Lopez Isnardi for his vital collaboration on the research and data collection in the preparation of this book.

My special thanks go to Kenneth Maxwell, the director of the Latin American Program at the Council on Foreign Relations, who organized the American study group and encouraged me to transform a background paper into a book. Thanks of another sort are owed to the Tinker Foundation, whose generous financial support made this project possible.

INTRODUCTION

One of the mysteries of the second half of the twentieth century is how Argentina, so rich in so many ways, has had such difficulty fulfilling its great potential. Argentina's postwar economic decline does not represent the case of a backward country failing to identify a path toward economic development. Instead, Argentina's failure represents the less common case of a relatively modern economy and society pursuing the wrong economic strategy and therefore being unable to cope with a major change in its environment.

There is no doubt that the international economic system and the global political environment changed to Argentina's disadvantage during the 1930s and 1940s. Argentina responded by adopting the policies of state capitalism, interventionism, and trade protectionism that had become popular, particularly in Europe, in the period between the two world wars. A mood of inward-looking nationalism and a somewhat adversarial view toward the workings of the new international economic order, which was sponsored by the United States and its allies, contributed to the country's increasing isolation. It is clear today that Argentina's response was not only awkward, given Argentina's relatively advanced economic position at the time, but also inadequate, given a world economy that was moving toward increased globalization and greater international interdependence.

The roots of Argentina's decline are to be found not only in the country's inability to respond to the new world environment. From 1930 to 1983, its political system was tainted by illegitimacy and severe instability. Again, the Argentine case differs from those of other developing societies characterized by political conflict and divisiveness. Its political instability was not the product of extreme poverty, unequal income distribution, or the lack of political participation by important and excluded segments of the population. On the contrary, there is ample evidence that Argentina's instability and conflict resulted from the struggle between organized social groups (for example, unionized workers, army officers, business sectors, government bureaucrats, etc.) to exert pressure through the state apparatus on the functioning of the political system in order to impose their diverse agendas on the rest of the society.

Originally one of Spain's poorest and most obscure American colonies, Argentina took up arms against the empire in 1810 and won its independence in 1816. Its armies of volunteers played decisive roles in the wars of independence of Chile, Peru, Uruguay, Paraguay, and Bolivia. After this splendid effort for liberation and the union of Latin America, Argentina entered a period of almost forty years of intermittent civil war, internal strife, political violence, economic backwardness, and international isolation.

In the second half of the nineteenth century, the country once again changed direction. A period of comprehensive institutional reform (1852–1860) laid the foundation for the development of an integrated national economy and political system. Argentina's economy, based on an agricultural export model, was fully integrated into the international economy, and the country enjoyed a privileged economic relationship with Europe, particularly with Great Britain. Argentina experienced a period of sustained economic, social, and institutional growth without parallel in Latin America, comparable to that then taking place in the countries that today are among the most advanced nations in the world.

Following World War I, Argentina ranked among the most advanced nations in terms of standard of living, and its political system operated within a framework of full democracy, an uncommon occurrence in those days. Its level of social development, measured by such indicators as home ownership and the number of university students and physicians per inhabitant, also placed it among the most advanced countries. By the beginning of World War II, most international analysts of economic and political affairs would have predicted a promising future for the young and prosperous nation. Nevertheless, during the following fifty years Argentina succumbed to political and institutional anarchy and economic decline.

From 1940 to 1983, the political system was highly unstable. This period was characterized by military coups, populist politics, and various forms of "restricted democracy," in which major political players were not allowed to participate formally in the electoral process. As a result, governments lacked the necessary legitimacy and popular backing to implement and sustain a democratic political system or to introduce the policies necessary to rekindle economic growth.

Argentina's postwar economic growth, from 1950 to 1990, was feeble. During this time, the country grew at an annual average per capita rate of only 0.5 percent and became increasingly isolated from the international economy. Its share of total international trade fell from

3 percent in 1929, to 2 percent in 1950, to 0.3 percent in 1990. Its standard of living lagged considerably in comparison to countries that were able to maintain sustained growth. Moreover, income distribution, after a period of brief improvement from 1945 to 1952, gradually deteriorated throughout the next four decades.

Among the group of the fifteen most advanced prewar nations, Argentina distinguished itself as the country with the worst economic performance and the greatest political instability of the postwar period. The same conclusion of relative failure can be drawn if we compare Argentina's performance with that of Brazil and Mexico, Latin America's two other large economies.

The postwar economic regime gave rise to a numb and rigid economy incapable of assimilating technology rapidly or reallocating production factors toward more productive activities. This economic regime was unable to foster stability and a growing level of prosperity for the population. Investment levels for the period from 1950 to 1988 were high, but the quality and efficiency of such investments were low, as evidenced by low levels of growth and productivity. While the real economy and its productive potential stagnated, a highly conflictive political system led to economic instability and encouraged speculation. This economic regime strongly exacerbated pre-existing political and social tensions, causing acute political and institutional instability, which increased uncertainty and further undermined the country's economic performance.

Argentina's economic and political crises extensively overlap. In recent decades, the Argentine government has lost its authority and legitimacy. The functional expansion of an "interventionist state" in the context of a "patrimonial state tradition"—wherein those who control the government believe they own the government—

TABLE 1. ARGENTINA'S PER CAPITA GDP AS A
PERCENTAGE OF THE GDP OF SELECTED COUNTRIES

	1913	1938	1950	1965	1989
Australia	57	60	57	51	37
Brazil	—	387	330	205	117
France	102	94	89	64	40
Germany	97	83	111	60	39
Italy	151	132	156	95	42
Japan	215	127	236	87	43
Mexico	—	177	149	120	104
South Korea	—	—	656	498	93
Spain	188	172	277	130	65
USA	64	59	44	40	27

Sources: Carlos Díaz Alejandro, *Essays on the Economic History of the
Argentine Republic* (New Haven: Yale University Press, 1970); Angus
Maddison, *Phases of Capitalist Development* (Oxford: Oxford Univer-
sity Press, 1982), and "A Comparison of Levels of GDP Per Capita in
Developed and Developing Countries, 1700-1980," *Journal of Eco-
nomic History* 43: 27–41, (March 1983); Robert Summers and Alan
Heston, "The Pen World Table: An Expanded Set of International
Comparison," 1950–1989," *The Quarterly Journal of Economics* (May
1991); Banco Central de la República Argentina, *Estimaciones An-
uales de la Oferta y Demanda Globales: Periodo 1980–1992* (Buenos
Aires: BCRA, April 1993).

had an altogether negative effect on economic organization. Increasingly, revenue came neither from productive work nor business innovation but from purely
speculative activities or those activities dependent upon
obtaining privileges from governments that were typically unstable and often illegitimate. This distorted the
system of incentives and diverted the business community from its organizing and innovating functions, redi-
recting it toward unproductive and speculative activities.

In-depth political reform began in 1983 with the
country's return to full democracy, and economic reform

was initiated with the Austral Plan in 1985. The wreckage of this plan and the subsequent catastrophe of hyper-inflation provoked a sharp rejection of the economic arrangements that had characterized Argentina in the postwar period, and the depth of the ensuing crisis paved the way for the major ongoing economic reform effort initiated in 1989.

The hyperinflationary crises of mid-1989 and early 1990 constitute a pivotal moment in Argentine history. It was then that Argentina finally managed to reverse the postwar trend that induced it to develop a semi-autarchic economic regime characterized by overextended, il-legitimate, and organizationally weak governments controlled by interest groups. The economic and institutional reforms now in progress are extensive, and, in their general outline, successful. However, decades of economic, political, and institutional decline and high uncertainty cannot be erased in a few years.

Many profound and irreversible structural changes have been initiated, including privatizations, deregulation, and restructuring of the foreign debt, although certain modifications may be necessary to correct some implementation problems. The Convertibility Plan, launched in March 1991, has yielded satisfactory macroeconomic results. With respect to such issues as liberalization of trade, tax reform, fiscal balance, labor reform, and restructuring of the domestic public debt, the Convertibility Plan has introduced significant changes and achieved important goals. But these reform efforts must be extended and completed if the new economic regime is to be consolidated and to provide a solid foundation for the positive political changes gradually introduced between 1983 and 1993. Argentina must also organize an efficient and independent civil service, upgrade its obsolete educational system, and create a vigorous export sector, thereby integrating its economy into the world economy, and reform the fiscal and organizational structure of its provincial governments.

This book contemplates the steps Argentina must take if it wishes, in the space of a generation, to become a prosperous, democratic, peaceful country fully assimilated into the group of most advanced nations. In the four chapters that follow, we will first examine the factors that determine economic growth and the paths followed by those nations that have joined the group of most advanced nations. In chapter 2, we will review the growth of Argentina's economy from 1870 to the present, focusing on the principal causes of stagnation and the acute crisis that began in the 1970s. In chapter 3, we will focus on the origins, objectives, and broad outlines of the economic reform process that is in progress and evaluate its results to date. In the final chapter, we will analyze the opportunities and difficulties presented by the ongoing reform process, evaluate the growth potential of the Argentine economy, and identify the main challenges that must be faced if Argentina is to recover its position in the group of most advanced nations.

The scope and purpose of this book does not permit a detailed analysis of major political issues. However, I am aware that the processes of reform and economic growth cannot be explained, at least in their primary causes, exclusively in economic terms, since economic processes are themselves interrelated with political, social, institutional, and international factors. Undoubtedly, political turmoil, divisiveness, and conflict, as well as the undisputed fact that Argentina was unable to create a stable and legitimate political system during the post–World War II period, are profoundly intertwined with the economic crisis and stagnation that have characterized Argentina's economy during the last decades.

Chapter 1

ECONOMIC GROWTH

When a society increases its production of goods and services, and saves and reinvests a portion of them, over time a gradual and sustained improvement in its standard of living occurs. Most economists agree that such economic growth is achieved by increasing productive resources—the so-called production factors—and/or by using them more efficiently.

Production factors include the quantity and quality of available land; physical capital, as in machinery, buildings, and inventory; human capital, or the available labor force and its education, training, experience, and motivation; and the availability of raw materials and nonrenewable resources. The accumulation of production factors depends on long-term demographic factors that affect the availability of human resources and the potential profitability of the production factors themselves. For example, physical investment increases in proportion to the expected return on capital, migration is related to wage differences among different regions or countries, and investment in education is related to expectations of increasing income. In other words, the potential profitability of production factors helps to determine the size and quality of investment, in terms of both physical and human capital. Improvement in the efficiency with which production factors are used mainly depends on the assimilation of technological innovation into the process of production, market size, and the quality of economic organization, as well as the interaction of these variables and their effects on the accumulation of the production factors cited above.

Economists long assumed that the key to economic development was capital accumulation. Beginning in the 1930s, however, with the pioneering works of Colin Clark, Simon Kuznets, and Joseph Schumpeter, they rediscovered the fundamental importance of technological innovation to growth processes.[1] While capital is the vehicle through which technological progress is usually disseminated, technological innovation increases the expected return on capital. The contribution of investment to production and to the rate of capital accumulation depends to a great extent on the business opportunities afforded by the new products, new processes, and cost reductions that result from technological innovation.

In the early postwar period, economists assumed that technological innovation was an important but exogenous variable with respect to economic growth, resulting from external scientific and technological advances. But a number of studies on generating and disseminating technological advances in various industries and activities established empirically that technological innovation responds to economic incentives, investment costs, and profit expectations, and brought about a profound change in their thinking.[2] Investment in research and development, and technological adaptation were seen to be important determinants of technological innovation,[3] which was seen, in turn, as the driving force of economic growth.[4]

Capital accumulation not only influences the swiftness with which new technologies are adopted but also contributes to the acquisition and dissemination of knowledge by the general public. Some technological advances incorporated in new machinery are transferred through on-the-job training of workers, and production costs usually decrease in relation to the degree to which management and labor are exposed to new technologies.[5] But there are also forms of technological progress that are not incorporated in physical capital, such as new management and marketing techniques, administration of working capital, financial organization, reorganization of production sequences, and personnel motivation.

Technological innovation, and the capacity of the population to absorb and adapt to technological change, are strongly dependent on the investment a society makes in the education and training of its human resources. Labor's resulting capacity to absorb new techniques reduces the risks associated with new investment, thereby generating higher levels of investment.[6]

In the case of "follower countries" (whose levels of capital and human productivity fall behind those of the most developed or advanced countries), investment in human capital and the level and quality of education are important factors in determining the speed with which these societies can assimilate the technological advances of more advanced countries.[7]

It is in this context that I would like to comment on the theory of "convergence," or "catch up." This theory holds that follower countries can speed up their growth and, over time, reach the productivity levels of the most advanced countries. They can assimilate, through capital accumulation, the most modern production processes—without having to incur the full costs of developing such technological advances—and "leap forward." When, according to this theory, productivity levels in the follower countries approach those of the advanced countries, their growth rates would slow down, also approaching those of the advanced countries. Since most countries with low levels of productivity have not begun a process of convergence, however, it remains to be explained why some countries have converged and others have not. The initial level of productivity appears to be a determining, though not the sole, factor. The institutional setting in which an economy develops, in particular the organization of the economy, also appears to be an important factor, as are the education and training of the labor force.[8]

One of the most interesting empirical phenomena in the history of economic growth, which serves to confirm the theory of convergence, is the acceleration of growth rates over time. The technological gap between "advanced" and "backward" countries, as well as the favorable opportunities offered by the international economy to disseminate technological innovations, especially with respect to the rapid growth of trade, improvements in transportation and communications, the growing role of multinational firms, and increased direct foreign investment, go a long way toward explaining the accelerated growth in recent years.

The importance of market size has been part of economic thought since Adam Smith concluded that "the division of labor is determined by the size of the market." In today's economic parlance, an increase in market size favors the efficiency of investment and of production factors by making it possible to take advantage of "economies of scale" (when the size of investment increases, there is more than a proportional increase of production) and "economies of specialization" (which accelerate cost reductions and increase the quantity and quality of production). The creation of integrated national markets, or free trade zones, or the promotion of greater integration with the international

TABLE 2. HISTORICAL COMPARISON OF GROWTH RATES OF
PER CAPITA GDP FOR SELECTED COUNTRIES

COUNTRY	PERIOD	ANNUAL GROWTH PER CAPITA (%)
Great Britain	1700–1820	0.4
France	1820–1870	1.0
United States	1820–1870	1.4
Argentina	1870–1929	1.6
Japan	1950–1980	6.7
Brazil	1965–1980	5.7
South Korea	1965–1989	8.4

Sources: The World Bank, *World Development Report 1991* (New York: Oxford University Press, 1991); A.G. Kenwood and A.L. Longheed, *The Growth of the International Economy, 1820–1990* (New York: Routledge, 1992); Angus Maddison, "A Comparison of Levels of GDP Per Capita in Developed and Developing Countries, 1700–1980," *Journal of Economic History*, 43: 27–41 (March 1983).

market are alternative mechanisms for increasing market size, promoting competition, improving resource allocation, and making future investment more productive through economies of scale and specialization.

A number of successful international experiences persuasively demonstrate the economic advantages of increasing market size. This is illustrated most recently by the creation of the European Community in 1957 and the success of the four export-oriented "Asian Tigers," and in the last century by the creation of bigger markets in the framework of new nation-states, such as Germany and Italy, or the reorganization of existing states, such as the United States and Argentina.

The quality of a country's economic organization— the institutional framework in which the economy functions—significantly affects the process of resource allocation, the speed with which new technologies are assimilated, and the rates of accumulation of physical and human capital. Economists have established that so far as private goods are concerned, markets operating freely and in a decentralized fashion efficiently distribute production factors among goods and services and develop a structure of goods and services that corresponds to the desires and values of the population. But markets are subject to certain distortions, including restrictions on competition, such as monopoly markets, or limitations on one's right to enjoy the fruits of one's labors. Such distortions, if they are not corrected, can reduce investment below optimum levels or channel resources to nonpriority activities.

Public goods, such as justice, public safety, defense, environmental protection, and general administration, or semi-public goods, such as education, public health, and research and development, are provided by the government. Public-sector decisions are made through collective decision-making mechanisms that involve the political system and the technocratic structures of the government. The efficiency of resource allocation[9] will fundamentally depend on the quality of decisions made governing the generation of resources, such as what taxes and fees to charge, and who should pay them, and how money should be spent. The production efficiency of the public sector will also depend on the government's ability to administer the resources at its disposal effectively and to optimize the quality of the goods and services it offers to society. Often, the government's managerial ability is low. The public sector may have seriously limited operational capabilities and access to information and is subject to the pressures of special interest groups.

Although these problems are inherent in government, their regularity and seriousness will depend on organizational quality and capacity in each particular case. Obviously, organizational capacity, as well as the stability, quality, and loyalty of public officials, and the nature of the relationship between officials and private and corporate interests, are decisive elements.

In the advanced countries, despite the intrinsic limitations noted above, the market and government have solved the difficult problems of organizing a complex economic society reasonably well. The opposite is true of the more backward countries, where market systems and government administration operate with severe defects and restrictions, which have seriously affected the accumulation of production factors and the efficiency with which they are used. Typically, a broad range of governmental measures—controls on prices, wages, and exchange rates; restrictions on international and domestic competition; and discriminatory subsidies and taxes—have undermined the conditions for competition and certainty that are necessary for the market to function properly. In the public sector, the institutional framework is seldom appropriate. Usually there is a substantial gap between the government's organizational capacity and its ambitious and often unrealistic objectives. This lack of agreement between aims and available means is one of the principal causes of a government's inefficiency in production and resource allocation.

Obviously, increments in the quantity and quality of physical and human capital, technological innovation, market size, and the quality of economic organization are profoundly interrelated, and all, in one way or another, help to determine a society's growth potential. Although economic prosperity can be reached through different avenues, in all countries that are now economically advanced, the acceleration of growth at first brought about disproportionate increases in domestic rates of savings and investment. In other words, growth gave rise to a "virtuous circle" that amplified and consolidated initial gains.[10] The relative share of GDP (gross domestic product) of principal sectors also changed significantly in all such countries during the process of modernization.[11] Agriculture's share of GDP fell below 10 percent. The manufacturing sector grew rapidly to account for a large share of GDP (typically between 20 and 35 percent). The behavior of the service sector was less consistent in the initial stages of growth, but it was the sector of greatest growth in the most advanced countries, where, with the growing importance of the subsectors of health, education, leisure, and the provision of such public goods and services as justice and public safety by the government, it came to represent 60 percent or more of GDP.

But there were also significant differences in the paths taken by countries now in the most advanced group. There is no single formula for promoting growth. Many countries, inspired by the propositions List and Hamilton put forward in the nineteenth century, have followed growth strategies based on protectionist policies geared toward developing the domestic industrial sector. In the nineteenth century, some countries with large national markets and significant levels of domestic competition, such as the United States and Germany, pursued this strategy, developing integrated and competitive industrial sectors. In the same period, other countries with smaller markets and less domestic competition, such as Italy and Spain, failed dismally. Between 1870 and 1913, annual average per capita growth for Germany and the United States was 1.6 percent and 2.1 percent, respectively, while for Italy and Spain, it was less than 1 percent. To illustrate the magnitude of this failure, it is enough to point out that Argentina's per capita manufacturing production in 1913 was 15 percent greater than Italy's and 50 percent greater than Spain's.[12]

In the postwar period, a large number of countries, most of them in the process of development (for example, Argentina, Brazil, Egypt, India, Nigeria, and Pakistan), have based their development strategies on massive import substitution. They believed that industrial protectionism would facilitate the transformation of the productive structure, elevate productivity levels, and reduce foreign dependence. It was only later that it was generally recognized that this model of "development from within" often gave rise to economies with low growth potential, high-cost industrial sectors, generally weakened rural sectors, a strong anti-export bias, and excessive government intervention.

Countries such as Japan and the four "Asian Tigers" (Hong Kong, Korea, Singapore, and Taiwan) fueled their postwar growth, despite the lack of natural resources, with the accelerated increase of exports of industrial manufactured goods, a process known as "export-led growth." This strategy was initially based on the utilization of a large "surplus of labor" (as a result of high levels of unemployment or underemployment)[13] and on an accelerated assimilation of foreign technologies into the processes of domestic production. The combination of an emphasis on exports, low wages, and the assimilation of readily available technology from the more advanced countries strongly increased their rates of return on physical and human capital and generated a large increase in the rates of accumulation of such capital. In the cases of Hong Kong and Singapore, this development took place in the framework of open, virtually unprotected economies. Japan, South Korea, and Taiwan combined selective protectionism and a strong bias in favor of exports. The fundamental difference between them and other postwar protectionist regimes is that they were strongly export oriented and their policies of promotion and protection were only transitory, which led to strong competition in the temporarily protected sectors. Furthermore, they had strong, well-organized governments and, at least in the initial stages, corporatist sectors that were not well organized and lacked the ability to control governmental policy.

Still other countries constructed modern and relatively diversified economies on the basis of developing and exporting primary natural resources. This was the case with Australia, New Zealand, Canada, and Argentina (up to 1940). These countries diversified their economic structures and modernized their trade, construction, and service sectors, in addition to developing large industrial sectors. In the case of Argentina, for example, the manufacturing sector's share of GDP increased from approximately 13 percent in 1900, to 20 percent in 1938.[14] By comparison, in 1988, the manufacturing sector accounted on average for 23.5 percent of GDP in the OECD countries.[15] In the beginning of the postwar period, all of these countries, with the exception of Argentina, were founding members of GATT (General Agreement on Tariffs and Trade) and with varying degrees of success became actively integrated in the flow of international trade and investment.

As we turn to a discussion of Argentina's postwar economic strategy and performance, it may be useful to note the case of Australia. While after World War II Australia protected its local industrial sector, it did not pursue the more extreme import-substitution industrial policies implemented by Argentina. Australia's more balanced development strategy did not seriously damage its natural-resource export potential. As a result, its per capita GDP in 1989 was almost three times greater than Argentina's, while the bulk of its exports over the last ten years were concentrated in raw materials of agricultural and mining origin, and industrial exports derived from the processing of these same raw materials.

Sweden and Denmark also constructed modern and relatively balanced societies during the twentieth century on the basis of comparative advantages in natural resources, supplemented by a major effort to develop human resources. Both countries chose to integrate themselves fully with the international economy. Their "openness coefficients," a measure of the degree of integration of a national economy in the world economy (exports, plus imports of real goods and services divided by 2, as a percentage of GDP) represented between 30 and 35 percent of their economies, a higher percentage than in most other advanced economies (e.g., the United States and Japan, about 10 percent; Australia, Italy, and Spain, about 20 percent; and France and Germany, about 25 percent). Both Sweden and Denmark developed specialized leading industrial sectors in areas directly or indirectly related to their comparative advantages.

At the end of the last century, Sweden had extensive forests and possessed great hydroelectric potential, but difficult climatic and geographic conditions obstructed transportation, communications, and economic activity in general. Nevertheless, the country became internationally competitive in such sectors as pulp and paper, specialty steels, and heavy transportation equipment. Swedish companies are internationally renowned for the production of goods and machinery and equipment used in mining, timber development, the production of pulp and paper, steel production, electricity generation, and telecommunications. Denmark developed its international competitiveness on the basis of agriculture and industries related to the products and by-products of that sector, consolidating its advantages through the development of highly trained workers. Denmark is internationally competitive in quality food products with high added value, as well as in machinery and products related to these industries, and in pharmaceuticals, vitamins, and medical equipment.

It is not enough, however, to explain why some countries grow rapidly (the process of convergence); it is also necessary to explain why some countries have sustained their economic progress over time, while many others, after initial success, have seen their relative positions deteriorate. Economic growth is not a balanced phenomenon. When an economy grows, certain sectors advance quickly, while others stagnate or decline. Some enterprises prosper, others undergo painful restructuring, and some disappear or go bankrupt. Some regions enjoy abundance, while others watch their active populations emigrate to centers of greater growth. Some professions and occupations offer good opportunities for increasing personal income rapidly, while in others the only increases are in unemployment. Growth is a process of constant assimilation of new technologies into production processes, which invariably forces the introduction of modifications in a country's economic and social structure. Though the economy may advance overall and average real wages may rise significantly, some sectors, regions, firms, and individuals will see their positions deteriorate, and will be compelled by progress to make changes and adjustments that they would not have made on their own initiative.

Permanent change is stressful, and in all societies activities in decline resist transformation. The social conflict between management and labor, protectionism, government regulations that inhibit competition, monopolistic or oligopolistic practices promoted by business groups, and intervention by the "sinecure state" (government by largesse) are some of the various mechanisms employed to delay or block the changes generated by economic growth. Sustained growth, on the other hand, requires the acceptance of change and competition.

The ability to sustain economic growth depends on complex social and political engineering. Politicians must be willing to operate in a setting of fairly rational macroeconomic policies, to correct errors when necessary, and not to resort to flagrant demagogic policies that offer short-term political payoffs but interfere with the mechanisms that promote growth in the long term. They must be able to articulate the interests of various groups and to resolve the inevitable social and political conflicts that are typical of all modern societies without putting at risk the mechanisms that facilitate capital accumulation, the assimilation of new technologies, and the efficient allocation of available resources.

Business people must be prepared to function in a competitive economic environment, in spite of the adverse effects of such competition on some of them. But they must be able to rely on the stability of the political and institutional framework, and on the likelihood that their contracts and property rights will be respected.

Government should promote competition and innovation in order to facilitate change, but it should also implement compensatory social policies that encourage the reallocation of resources toward productive activities, while minimizing the social costs invariably produced by economic growth. It should execute this compensatory function while maintaining a reasonable degree of autonomy and independence, not as a vehicle for the distribution of sinecures and privileges. Furthermore, the government should be perceived by the majority in a society to be working for the common interest, not as the tool of special interests.

Sustained growth also depends in the long term on establishing a balance between investment and consumption and between productivity, profitability, and wages. It requires the majority of the population to support policies that foster change and economic restructuring and to understand that through wage increases workers will share in the benefits that result from technological innovation and greater productive efficiency. In developed countries, as investors gained confidence in the stability of the institutional framework, living standards for the general public increased. This, in turn, conferred stability on labor relations and favored the continuation of the process of productive restructuring brought about by growth, despite the social frictions, dislocations, unemployment, and business failures such change necessarily entails. Success in sustaining growth over time depends on a country's ability to create policies that favor the accumulation of physical and human capital and promote an economic organization that favors the efficient use of resources while simultaneously meeting these complicated political and institutional challenges.

An objective assessment of Argentina's ongoing economic reform program and the prospects for growth of Argentina's economy must be based on an accurate analysis of the problems that have afflicted Argentine society and the underlying causes that have given rise to Argentina's stagnation and decline in recent decades. To this end, in the next chapter we will examine Argentina's economic performance from 1870 to 1989, focusing on the causes of "growth and convergence" from 1870 to 1938, "relative lag" from 1940 to 1973, and "stagnation" from 1973 to 1989.

Chapter 2

ARGENTINA'S ECONOMIC PERFORMANCE FROM 1870 TO 1989

Let us begin with some key statistical data to allow the reader to analyze Argentina's economic performance and draw comparisons with other countries.

The data in table 3 reveal Argentina's economic position relative to a selected group of countries between 1870 and 1989. From this table we can also obtain the ranking of the wealthiest countries between 1870 and 1989. Obviously, a comparison of per capita income among countries over a period of 120 years is subject to numerous errors and problems of consistency, and there are problems inherent in comparing figures for purchasing power and currency conversion. But even though the data are not entirely reliable, I am confident that the general conclusions derived from the data are valid and that such a comparative approach provides a useful framework for considering the Argentine economy's historical performance, current standing, and prospects.

A synoptic view of growth in Argentina for the period from 1901 to 1990 in terms of GDP and per capita GDP per five-year period is presented in figure 1 (see also table 1 in the appendix).

TABLE 3. EVOLUTION OF PER CAPITA GDP FOR THE
WEALTHIEST COUNTRIES BETWEEN 1870 AND 1989
(DOLLARS IN 1989 PURCHASING POWER)[a]

	1870	1913	1938	1950	1965	1980	1989
Argentina	1432	2739	3107	3602	4422	5674[b]	5675[b]
Australia	3691	4845	5204	6274	8583	11830	15266
Austria	1442	2758	4892	2948	6213	11006	13063
Belgium	2184	3415	4615	4384	6904	11673	13313
Brazil	—	—	803	1092	2158	4895	4832[c]
Canada	1692	4004	4215	6474	9360	14456	18635
Chile	—	1895	2069	2357	3000	4488	4987
Denmark	1697	3311	4360	5450	8633	12716	13751
Finland	971	2022	3559	3722	6678	10832	14598
France	1481	2691	3317	4029	6918	11730	14164
Germany	1404	2819	3727	3247	7332	13037	14507
Great Britain	2288	3605	4297	4846	6901	8844	13732
Holland	2120	3055	3680	4525	7340	11097	13351
Hong Kong	—	—	—	—	3764	9064	14450
Ireland	1260	1934	—	2828	4286	6705	7481
Italy	1318	1811	2350	2305	4676	8497	13608
Japan	726	1272	2444	1523	5097	10461	13283
Mexico	—	—	1753	2420	3696	6265	5436
Norway	1277	2232	3787	4876	7640	12435	16838
New Zealand	1884	3119	—	6101	8798	9072	11155
Portugal	1223	1392	—	1142	2308	5464	6259
Russia	786	1179	1905	2552	5197	—	6270
Singapore	—	—	—	—	2830	8932	11334
South Korea	—	—	—	549	887	2242	6117
Spain	—	1457	180	1300	3390	5590	8723
Sweden	1070	2566	4405	5742	9397	12664	14817
Switzerland	2147	3584	5543	6178	9902	12268	18590
Taiwan	—	—	—	630	1430	4119	6210[c]
USA	1749	4307	5260	8191	11052	14938	20998

Sources: Carlos Díaz Alejandro, *Essays on the Economic History of the Argentine Republic* (New Haven: Yale University Press, 1970); Angus Maddison, *Phases of Capitalist Development* (Oxford: Oxford University Press, 1982), and "A Comparison of Levels of GDP Per Capita in Developed and Developing Countries, 1700–1980," *Journal of Economic History* 43: 27–41, (March 1983); Robert Summers and Alan Heston, "The Pen World Table: An Expanded Set of International Comparison, 1950–1989," *The Quarterly Journal of Economics* (May 1991); Banco Central de la República Argentina, *Estimaciones Anuales de la Oferta y Demanda Globales: Periodo 1980–1992* (Buenos Aires: BCRA, April 1993).

[a] To facilitate the comparison, the original data (which was calculated on the basis of U.S. relative prices) has been transformed into 1989 values using as an adjustment the wholesale price index of the United States for the corresponding period.

[b] For Argentina, the values for 1980 and 1989 come from the new National Accounts published by the Central Bank in 1993. The equivalent value in the "Penn World Table" (based on the old National Accounts) for 1989 was estimated at $4.310.

[c] Data for 1988.

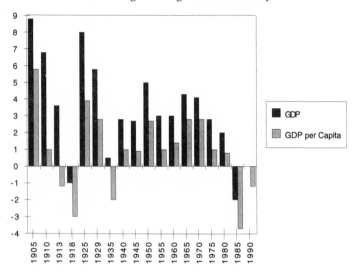

FIGURE 1. AVERAGE RATE OF GROWTH OF GDP AND PER CAPITA GDP (IN FIVE-YEAR PERIODS, 1901–1990)

Source: Author's treatment. This graph reconstructs a long series of GDP figures, based on CEPAL and Central Bank studies on national accounts. Although these figures are not homogeneous, I believe that the data are, in broad strokes, representative of events that took place in Argentina's economy between 1901 and 1990.

"CONVERGENCE" (1870–1938)

In 1870, Argentina's standard of living represented approximately 53 percent of the average for the three countries with highest per capita income (Australia, Great Britain, and Switzerland). From the available data (see table 3), we can estimate that at this time Argentina ranked twelfth among the 22 nations with highest per capita GDP. The economic position of Argentina in 1870 should not surprise us. It is explained in part by an abundance of natural resources and a small population.

Also studies have shown that, at the beginning of the Industrial Revolution, differences in standards of living between countries that did and did not take part in the revolution were small. In other words, most of the present gap between the standards of living of the most developed countries and those of the rest of the world is a result of the economic growth that took place after the Industrial Revolution.[1]

Growth rates in the nineteenth century and the first part of the twentieth century were small compared to those of nations that grew rapidly after World War II. It is estimated that average per capita growth during the period from 1870 to 1913 was 1.1 percent for Great Britain, 1.4 percent for France, 1.6 percent for Germany, and 2.1 percent for the United States.[2] From 1870 to 1913 (a period of rapid growth in the international economy), the average growth in Argentina's per capita GDP was 1.7 percent, higher than the rates of most of the advanced nations.[3] During this period, the country experienced accelerated growth and convergence, its levels of productivity and standard of living gradually approaching those of the most advanced nations of the time.

The political basis for this economic growth was laid between 1853 and 1870, when a liberal constitution was approved and profound institutional changes were introduced, laying solid foundations for the development of an integrated economy and a national political system. A federal civil administration, a judicial system, and a professional army were created for the first time. Until 1916, the country was governed by a conservative coalition that had strong roots in rural areas and in the provinces. This coalition administered the governmental apparatus and controlled the political system, which had a republican structure. Civil rights and individual liberties and freedom of the press were generally maintained, and the opposition was able to voice dissent and participate in the political process (but was able to win elections only occasionally). The conservative alliance, which gained its support from landowners and the fast-growing urban business community, was able to maintain control through a system in which the president selected his successor with the consent of the most important provincial governors. Elections were won by limiting the number of potential voters and, when required, through fraud.

The incorporation of Argentina's economy into the international economy was fostered by increased exports of agricultural products: first wool and leather, then grains and meat. The significant growth of these industries led to expanded transportation (railroads and ports), trade, and construction sectors. Industrial development up until World War I was modest, except in agricultural industries directed toward exports (for example, frozen meat and grain mills), the metallurgical industry (supplying railroads), and industries linked to construction. Nevertheless, the constant increase in population, fueled by waves of immigration, gradually created a large domestic consumer market that encouraged the establishment of manufacturing in the production of food, clothes, and perishable goods.[4] In 1913, Argentina's per capita GDP was approximately 62 percent of that of the three nations with the highest per capita GDP (Australia, the United States, and Canada). During World War I, growth stagnated, a predictable result in a dynamic economy strongly dependent on foreign trade with the warring European nations. On the other hand, the war hampered imports of a variety of products, which acted as a stimulus to the development of domestic textile, chemical, and metallurgical industries.

In 1912, rapid modernization, as well as growing pressure from new social groups—particularly urban workers and the middle class—led President Roque Saenz Peña, a Conservative, to substantially reform the controversial electoral system. The male vote was made universal, obligatory, and secret. This reform opened up the political system and allowed the main opposition, the Radical party, to win key elections and control the presidency between 1916 and 1930. From 1919 to 1929, Argentina's economy enjoyed a golden age and grew at an annual average rate of almost 6.8 percent (3.4 percent in terms of per capita GDP), certainly an international record in those days (see table 1 in the appendix). It is important to emphasize that this rapid economic growth was achieved within an entirely democratic framework—a privilege enjoyed by only a small group of nations.

In 1930, a right-wing military coup, the first to succeed in nearly 80 years of civilian government, eventually allowed the Conservative party to regain power, which it maintained until 1943, thanks to an alliance with a dissident faction of the Radical party and to electoral fraud. During the 1930s, Argentina's economy suffered from the impact of the Great Depression, which reduced the volume of international trade and levels of economic activity around the world. The depression particularly affected relative prices for Argentine exports as the terms of trade deteriorated. Between 1930 and 1935, GDP fell 2.1 percent per year, recovering at an annual average rate of 1.1 percent between 1935 and 1940 (see table 1 in the appendix). Although this was certainly a setback, Argentina did not lose its relative economic position since the depression was international and severely affected all advanced nations. In 1938, Argentina's per capita GDP represented 57 percent of per capita GDP of the three most advanced nations

(Switzerland, the United States, and Australia), and the country ranked fifteenth in per capita GDP among the most advanced nations.

Several indicators confirm Argentina's economic progress between 1920 and 1938. The investment rate in the manufacturing sector from 1923 to 1929 was the highest between the years 1900 and 1990. From 1920 to 1939, direct foreign investment in Argentina was concentrated in the industrial sector. The annual average for direct foreign investment during this period was 3.7 percent of GDP,[5] and major international companies such as Nestlé, Colgate Palmolive, Firestone, Johnson and Johnson, Goodyear, Dupont, Otis Elevators, R.C.A., I.T.T., Lever Bros, Michelin, Phillips, General Electric, Pirelli, and Osram began operating in the country.[6] Approximately 55 percent of all automobiles in South America were in Argentina, and Argentina accounted for more than 40 percent of South America's railroads, 63 percent of its postal services, and 64 percent of its radios and newspapers, and it spent 65 percent of the total amount allocated for education in the region.[7] In 1938, approximately 65 percent of the manufactures for final consumption were produced locally.[8] The illiteracy rate fell from 80 percent in 1870, to 25 percent in 1929, to 13 percent in 1947.[9] Real wages for urban and rural workers were comparable, or at least close, to those in the developed countries of western Europe.[10]

However, the 1930s represented a significant turning point in the institutional and economic organization of the country. The military coup d'état of 1930 and the subsequent period of electoral fraud broke the continuity of the democratic system. The new regime was not totalitarian—that is, it did not abrogate civil rights and liberties. But the change of regime strengthened the power of corporatist groups and created a new dimension of uncertainty, divisiveness, and political and social conflict that would have profound consequences for decades to come.

Argentina also began to isolate itself from the international economy. Its average openness coefficient dropped from 33 percent in the 1920s, to 25 percent in the 1930s.[11] Moreover, the role of the state as a producer of goods and services and as a regulator of economic activities began to grow rapidly. Public spending by the federal, provincial, and municipal governments, which represented approximately 11 percent of GDP between 1915 and 1919, increased steadily to approximately 21 percent of GDP from 1935 to 1939.[12]

"RELATIVE LAG" (1940–1973)

These three decades were characterized by profound social and political conflict. The military coup that ended the Conservative party's rule in 1943 was carried out by the most nationalistic and inward-looking elements of the officer corps. Within that group, Colonel Juan Domingo Perón, a career army officer with a brilliant political mind and strong nationalistic and populist ideas, gained gradual ascendancy by recognizing the political potential offered by a growing, but still disorganized, labor force. He and his attractive wife, Eva, mesmerized a large segment of the Argentine population and gradually, between 1943 and 1946, took control of the armed forces and the trade union movement. Perón became president in 1946. The Perón government, which was popularly elected, carried out a major redistribution of national income that benefited, at least in the short run, the low-income sectors of society. It established the foundations of a powerful welfare state (managed by the government and the trade unions) and further extended the role of the state through nationalizations and a high degree of government intervention in foreign and local trade, banking, and insurance. The government received its main support from the army, the enlarged state bureaucracy, some local entrepreneurs (who benefited from protectionist policies and government support), and the trade unions, which were sponsored by the government and became the main beneficiaries of its policies. Perón enjoyed wide popular support even though the civil rights and individual liberties of his opponents were not always respected, the press was controlled, and the political activities of the opposition (the Radical, Conservative, and Socialist parties) were curtailed.

Perón was deposed by a combined military and civilian coup in 1955. Until 1973, when he returned to power briefly, Argentina alternated between anti-Perónist military and civilian governments. The politics of the period were highly unstable. During this eighteen-year span there were ten different presidents (five civilian and five military), who were unable to establish the legitimate political system that Argentina needed in order to resume genuine and sustained growth and institutional modernization. During this period of political instability, Argentina's economy grew at lower rates than the economies of the more advanced nations and of a group of developing countries that were able to grow steadily. Argentina's economic performance from 1940 to 1973 was characterized by modest per capita growth, increasing inflation, substantial government deficits, and a closed domestic economy.

During the 1940s, Argentina's economy grew at an annual average per capita rate of approximately 1.9 percent, and the country began to lose its position relative to the more advanced nations. Per capita GDP fell from 57 percent of that of the three most advanced

TABLE 4. ECONOMIC PERFORMANCE INDICATORS (1940–1973)

	1940/45	1946/50	1951/55	1956/60	1961/65	1966/73
GDP Growth (annual avg. %)	2.6	5.0	3.0	3.0	4.4	3.7
Population (millions, end of period)	15.4	17.2	18.9	20.6	22.3	25.2
Per Capita GDP Growth %	0.9	2.8	1.0	1.3	2.8	2.1
Investment/GDP (annual avg. %)	17.8	25.2	16.8	17.1	19.8	19.7
M3/GDP %	52.4	54.3	42.6	33.3	23.1	26.3
Consumer Price Inflation (annual avg. %)	5.6	20.0	18.2	38.3	23.2	22.8
Public Expenditure/GDP (annual avg. %)	21.0	31.4	30.0	26.2	24.7	24.5
Fiscal Deficit/GDP (annual avg. %)	4.5	10.8	7.8	5.2	8.9	3.1
Openness Coefficient (annual avg. %)	11.7	12.2	10.2	10.7	10.0	9.5

Sources: CEPAL, *El Desarrollo Económico de la Argentina* (México City: CEPAL 1959); IEERAL "Estadísticas de la Evolución económica de la Argentina, 1913–1984," *Estudios* (July-September 1986); and Banco Central de la República Argentina, *Memorias Anuales* (1940–1974).

9

nations (the United States, Canada, and Australia) in
1938, to 51.6 percent in 1950, despite the fact that the
country did not participate in World War II.

Average annual growth for Argentina's per capita
GDP stood at 1.1 percent in the 1950s and 2.4 percent in
the 1960s. The annual average inflation rate rose from
approximately 13 percent in the 1940s, to 28 percent in
the 1950s, to 33 percent between 1960 and 1973. The
economy began to demonetize and the money supply,
defined as M3 (currency, deposit accounts, savings accounts, and fixed-term deposits), which represented 50
percent of GDP between 1929 and 1950, gradually de-
creased to roughly 25 percent of GDP in the 1960s.

Public spending (federal, provincial, and municipal) increased from 21 percent of GDP in 1939, to 32
percent in 1950, and was reduced to 25 percent of GDP
in the 1960s and 1970s.[13] The public sector's participation in the economy grew much more than indicated by
these figures because of the increasing role of public
enterprises (nearly 15 percent of GDP in 1960) and the
weight of government regulations, as well as the expanding participation of the government in retirement plans
(nearly 7 percent of GDP in 1960), banking, and foreign
trade. Fiscal deficits were very high throughout, but
especially from 1946 to 1965, when the average annual
deficit accounted for more than 8 percent of GDP.

Investment held steady at fairly high levels in the
1950s and 1960s, representing approximately 17 percent
and 20 percent of GDP, respectively. Yet an important
part of this investment was promoted by the state
through credit or tax exemptions or consisted of direct
public investment—public-sector investment, including
government-owned firms, accounted for approximately
7 percent of GDP from 1950 to 1973.[14]

Argentina fell from fifteenth place among the

wealthiest countries in 1938 to nineteenth place in 1965, when its per capita GDP accounted for 44 percent of that of the three most advanced nations (the United States, Switzerland, and Sweden). In comparison to growth rates for other countries in the nineteenth century and the first 40 years of the twentieth century, Argentina's growth rates for the 1940–1973 period seem reasonable. Nevertheless, if we compare its rates with those of the advanced countries and a small group of "newly industrialized countries" (NICs) during these years, we are forced to see this period as one of "relative lag" in the country's growth (see table 5).

The growth rates of the small group of nations that grew rapidly in the postwar period were much higher than their growth rates in preceding periods: after World War II growth became easier. The Western developed nations, Japan, and a small group of NICs took advan-

TABLE 5. RATE OF GDP GROWTH FOR ARGENTINA AND SELECTED COUNTRIES BETWEEN 1950 AND 1990 (IN %)

Decade	1950	1960	1970	1980
Argentina	3.0	4.3	2.6	−1.0
Brazil	6.8	8.5	7.9	2.9
Germany	8.8	4.5	2.4	2.0
Italy	6.3	5.7	3.8	2.2
Japan	8.9	12.2	4.1	4.2
Mexico	6.1	7.0	6.6	0.6
South Korea	—	9.5	8.2	9.3
Singapore	—	9.2	9.0	7.1
Spain	—	7.6	3.7	2.9
USA	3.3	3.8	2.8	2.5

Sources: International Monetary Fund, "International Financial Statistics" (Washington: *Annual Reports*, 1970–1993).

tage of the many opportunities that the postwar period of reconstruction offered. They benefited from the accelerated growth of international trade and the opportunity to quickly incorporate, at reasonable cost, sophisticated technological advances as well as the most modern methods of management, marketing, and business organization. Though there is no single explanation for the substantial increases in their growth rates, a number of elements were significant. In the case of the nations that were already economically advanced (the countries of western Europe and Japan), the depression, with its low rates of investment, and/or the destruction caused by World War II resulted in the strong productivity increases of the postwar reconstruction period. The initial availability of a stock of previously unused technological innovations also contributed significantly to postwar growth.[15] These countries were able to bring into production a large backlog of unexploited technology, particularly methods of production and of industrial and commercial organization already in use in the United States at the end of the war but not yet employed in the other countries of the West and Japan.

In addition, for the losers, particularly Germany and Japan, defeat meant a break with the prewar domestic organizational structures and institutions that had hindered competition, technological innovation, and sustained growth. Among the factors that had impeded their growth were the monopolies and oligopolistic pacts that regulated competition, the growth of state interventionism, and the broad expansion of protectionist policies with respect to international trade. Mancur Olson has analyzed in detail how such an economic environment tends to reinforce organized interest groups that end up dominating the economic and political structures of a society.[16] Such nonproductive economic behavior ("unproductive profit-seeking activities") diminishes the ability of a society to adapt to its own growth and, over time, discourages innovation and slows the rate of growth.[17] The combination of large technological gaps, relatively educated and strongly motivated populations eager to improve their income after the war's sacrifices, appropriate institutional structures (stable political systems and market economies), the dismantling of monopolistic structures, the liberalization of multilateral trade, and stable strategic and military alliances with the United States provided firm ground for a rapid increase in technological innovation, productivity, and growth in Japan and Western Europe.

In the case of the NICs that grew rapidly in the postwar period, all of them, though at different rates and with different strategies, took advantage of opportunities offered by the international economy. Growth was connected in every case to a significant increase in exports (mainly manufactures) to the most developed countries, which was facilitated by the liberalization of trade under GATT. All of these economies were actively motivated to incorporate sophisticated technologies (already in use in the most advanced countries) in their economic processes. Assimilation of these technologies took place by various means, notably through foreign investment, particularly on the part of large multinational corporations (in Brazil, Mexico, Singapore, and Taiwan), through the extensive use of cross-border production agreements (subcontracting in-bond industry, or *maquiladoras*) with the most advanced countries (on the part of South Korea, Hong Kong, Mexico, and Taiwan), through the acquisition and purchase of patents and licenses, and through copying or reproducing products and processes already in use in the most advanced countries.

All of these NICs developed friendly, nonadversarial political relationships with the most economically advanced countries and often received preferential treatment in return, particularly from the United States. It is also important to note that a strategy for economic growth based on an active participation in international trade tends, given certain basic levels of development and training of human resources, to favor and accelerate the incorporation of new technologies into the domestic economy. Firms that become involved in exporting are committed to improving their product and to introducing new technologies so as to be able to compete in international markets. Competing imports introduce new varieties of products, squeezing the profit margins of domestic producers (often monopolistic or oligopolistic) and, through the pressure of competition, force firms to innovate and invest.[18]

Finally, throughout the period in question, these NICs maintained fairly rational macroeconomic policies, quickly correcting any major fiscal or monetary excesses. To a certain extent, they invested in the development of human resources, expanding elementary and high school programs and encouraging scientific and technical training, either at home or abroad. And they enjoyed stable political systems that facilitated the continuity of economic policies and reduced levels of social conflict.

There is no doubt that the globalization of the international economy—through trade, foreign investment, capital markets, and personal contacts facilitated by new transportation and telecommunication technologies—has been the most important means of disseminating advanced technologies. The NICs were able to take advantage of these opportunities for rapid growth. Unfortunately, Argentina was relatively isolated from the international economy from 1940 onward and did not participate in this process of technological dissemination to any great extent. In addition to the political turmoil that characterized Argentina during this period, its isolation was one of two fundamental reasons for its modest economic performance from 1940 to 1973, as well as for the decline it experienced in the two following decades. The failure of the government to carry out its overly ambitious tasks was the second.

Isolation

Two events during the 1940s defined the new spirit of the times and symbolized the confusion of the Argentine decision-making elite about political and economic international development, as well as the determining factors of long-term economic growth. The first was the military coup d'état in June 1943, which was carried out to prevent a break in diplomatic relations with the Axis countries at a time when it was clear to most observers that the Allies would win the war. Beginning in November 1942, the Axis nations had suffered major defeats on all fronts—in North Africa, southern Europe, and the Soviet Union—and Mussolini resigned and was arrested in July 1943. Argentina had initially adopted a neutral position during World War II, in accordance with its longstanding diplomatic tradition of noninvolvement in other countries' affairs. Although the majority of the public and most of the business and political establishment supported the Allies, pro-Axis feelings were strong in the military and among various right- and left-wing nationalist groups that had begun to flourish during the 1930s. The second defining event was Argentina's decision in 1947 not to participate in GATT. It should be remembered that one of the pivotal resolutions adopted by the GATT signatories during the early years was to exclude the agricultural sector from multilateral trade liberalization programs implemented during the postwar period. Argentina's reluctance to sign the agreement and delayed participation in the negotiations is therefore surprising if we consider that, in the mid-1930s, Argentina's share of world agricultural exports stood at 50 percent for corn, 40 percent for meat, and 20 percent for wheat.[19]

It was the view of the administrations of this period, unfortunately shared by segments of the main opposition parties and by a significant sector of public opinion, that the new postwar economic order, defined by the Bretton Woods agreement (creating the International Monetary Fund and the World Bank) and GATT, favored the interests and aspirations of the United States and the most advanced nations at the expense of Argentina.

The isolationist mood that pervaded Argentina's politics and economic policies since the 1940s had its origins in the disturbances in the international system created by the depression and the war. These experiences, in particular the reduction in exports and foreign capital inflows, profoundly weakened the close commercial and financial alliance between Argentina and Great Britain and seemed to create a world economic system disadvantageous to Argentina's economic interests. International trade fell dramatically, both in terms of volume and prices, and capital inflows, which had been so important for Argentina between 1880 and 1930, nearly disappeared. In particular, Britain's trade policy shift from "free trade" toward "imperial preferences" penalized Argentina and was deeply resented as unfair and discriminatory.

Argentina turned to state interventionism and protectionism in the economic arena and nationalism, populism, and militarism in the political arena—mistaken strategies in response to the new world environment. Argentina challenged the most advanced countries, intensely criticizing real and imaginary flaws in the new economic order favored by the United States and its allies, and countered the Bretton Woods multilateral liberalization policies with protectionist bilateral policies. The rejection of multilateralism, trade liberalization, and international financial coordination (Argentina was not a member of the International Monetary Fund or the World Bank until the late 1950s) expressed an increasingly isolationist and adversarial spirit. And Argentina rejected not only the new international economic order, but the market and competition as mechanisms for resource allocation as well. This militaristic and nationalistic resurgence of the 1940s had anti-American overtones that hindered relations with the United States, which, ironically, was attempting to recreate a world economic order based on the principles of multilateral trade and finance that had benefited Argentina in the past.

To understand the significance of these developments, it is important to remember that in 1938 Argentina's per capita GDP was four times greater than that of Brazil and Mexico, approximately 40 percent and 23 percent greater than that of Italy and Japan, respectively, and only 10 percent and 20 percent lower than that of France and Germany, respectively (see table 1), and that the level of social development was relatively advanced, as indicated by the strong postwar European immigration numbers (approximately 500,000 European immigrants arrived in the country between 1947 and 1951).[20]

Argentina was the only one of the twenty most economically advanced nations that completely rejected the new international economic order and promoted a dichotomy between rich countries and poor countries, even though its standard of living and productive structure clearly placed it in the first group. An objective and dispassionate analysis of world circumstances on the part of its leaders would have set the country on an entirely different course, and Argentina could have joined the select group of nations that benefited from the expansion of the international economy over the course of the following decades.

Consistent with its isolationist and adversarial outlook, Argentina's domestic economic policy entailed the adoption of an industrialization strategy of import substitution, or development from within, aimed at creating an industrial sector geared to satisfying domestic demand and at redistributing wealth from the agricultural sector to the urban sector. This strategy sought simultaneously to diversify Argentina's productive structure, raise productivity, improve the distribution of wealth, and decrease foreign dependency.[21]

The strategy produced initial benefits, particularly for the protected sectors, but over time it resulted in an economy of low growth potential.[22] The protected industrial sector grew in the 1950s and 1960s at annual average rates of 4 percent and 5.6 percent respectively. But the strategy prevented the industrial sector from benefiting from the economies of scale and specialization that were decisive for other nations,[23] and created an industrial structure with high relative costs by international standards, excessively diversified in its array of products, with small-scale industrial plants and a strong dependency on imported intermediate goods, capital goods, and technology.

The strategy also discriminated against the agricultural sector. The government's foreign exchange and tax policies, which reduced investment levels and hindered technological innovation, led to diminishing growth in production and fewer agricultural exports.[24] The strategy prejudiced the exporting potential of the domestic economy in the industrial sector as well. The high relative costs produced by excessive protection of the domestic market, the growing inefficiencies of state administration vis-à-vis physical and institutional infrastructure—ports and railroads, customs, and the central bank—and many cumbersome fiscal, labor, and regulatory policies weakened the domestic economy's export potential. The average annual growth rate of Argentine exports from 1950 to 1970 was only 2.1 percent.

The Functional Crisis of the Interventionist State

Argentina's adversarial stance with respect to the international economic system, its self-imposed isolation, and its strategy of import substitution were key factors in the deterioration of the country's economy. The other main factor was the serious incongruence between the organizational capacity of the Argentine state apparatus and the ambitious objectives and multiple functions that it had adopted.

Some economists, especially the so-called Neostructuralists, have asserted that Argentina's experience between 1940 and 1970 was not very different from that of other similarly semi-industrialized and dependent countries.[25] In the opinion of these analysts, the process of growth in such countries must be guided by the state. The interventionist state replaces the mechanisms of the market in the determination of relative prices and costs, sectoral profitability, and income distribution. They believe that interventionist policies geared towards controlling the main prices of the economy in order to accelerate industrialization (for example, export restrictions, multiple exchange rates, income policies), changing the sys-

TABLE 6. EVOLUTION OF EXPORTS OF ARGENTINA,
AND A GROUP OF SELECTED COUNTRIES, 1950–1970
(MILLIONS OF DOLLARS)

	1950	1960	1970	AVERAGE ANNUAL GROWTH RATE (%)
Argentina	1,178	1,079	1,773	2.1
Asia NICs[a]	1,731	2,022	6,331	6.7
Australia	1,668	1,997	4,623	5.2
Brazil	1,359	1,268	2,739	3.6
Chile	289	488	1,246	7.6
EEC[b]	14,837	31,465	81,532	8.9
Germany	1,993	11,415	34,228	15.3
Italy	1,206	3,654	13,185	12.7
Japan	825	4,055	19,318	17.1
Mexico	532	765	1,313	4.6
Spain	389	725	2,390	9.5
USA	10,282	20,601	43,241	7.5

Sources: International Monetary Fund, "International Financial Statistics"
(Washington: *Annual Reports*, 1970–1993); "General Agreement on
Trade and Tariffs," International Trade Statistics (Geneva: *Annual
Reports*, 1950–1980).
[a] Hong Kong, Singapore, South Korea, and Taiwan.
[b] Not including Germany.

tem of incentives (for example, promoting specific exports, sectors and/or regions), and transferring wealth between sectors (forced savings) are necessary prerequisites in hastening the development and consolidating the productive structure of countries like Argentina.

Although these policies have worked (with different degrees of success) in other economies that have grown rapidly, they have not done so in Argentina. The possibility of success for social and economic policies with a distinct state-interventionist tone depends strongly on the institutional framework in which such policies are carried out, the level of organization of the governmental apparatus and the nature and orientation of the economic policies adopted.[26]

Interventionist policies worked for a time in postwar Japan and in South Korea after 1962 because both countries had very weak sectoral interests (a result of military defeat and, in Japan's case, of the liberalizing policies implemented by the American occupying forces and, in Korea's case, of the extensive Japanese and, later, American occupations).[27] Both countries, as a result of tradition in Japan and circumstances in South Korea, had strong and fairly well-organized governments. In general, government interventions were shaped by a long-term pro-market philosophy, encouraging domestic competition in the protected or subsidized sectors of a large national market in Japan and a strong export orientation in South Korea. In addition, these promotional subsidies and protections were only temporary and rarely applied to declining sectors or businesses with problems.

Nothing could be farther from the institutional framework of contemporary Argentina, where interventionist policies had a counterproductive effect. They first stalled and then blocked the country's growth while producing, in the 1970s and 1980s, a crisis of stagnation and deterioration without parallel in contemporary economic history among countries with the relative importance and size of Argentina that likewise did not suffer from the consequences of war on their territory.

The Argentine government was historically weak and never enjoyed more than a small degree of autonomy and independence. During its phase of "national organization" (1852–1880), a central power was consolidated, superseding the powers of the *caudillos* (local bosses). A constitution was written and a national integrated market created, and a federal army, a judicial system, and a state bureaucracy were formed. Yet, despite this initial success, in the ensuing hundred years, the Argentine government was unable to create an independent civil administration with a well-paid and well-trained core of officials loyal to the state who could provide successive administrations with technical assistance for administering policies in the public interest. The classic cases of fostering bureaucratic excellence are Japan and France, but Brazil and Mexico, discussed below, more clearly illustrate Argentina's problem.

The modern Argentine state continued to operate as a patrimonial state. The state as the "king's patrimony," to be administered directly or through his representatives at his discretion, was a leftover from Argentina's colonial history. The idea that those who are in power consider themselves owners of the state apparatus inevitably leads to the practices of patronage and cronyism in recruiting public officials. Consequently, politicization, corruption, and the predominance of personal interest over the public good came to characterize the Argentine state.

The growth of the interventionist state in the postwar period considerably aggravated the situation by enabling badly informed, inadequately paid, and poorly motivated officials to make a broad range of decisions that generated high costs and privileges for the private sector. It is not surprising that government corruption was widespread and control was practically impossible. The personal corruption of these officials was nothing but the exercise, on a smaller, individualized scale, of the same patrimonial view of the state. A system for the selection, promotion, and training of public officials did not exist in Argentina before 1943, either at the federal or provincial levels. The only requirement for becoming a public official was that one had to be at least eighteen years old. In reality, every public institution enjoyed the freedom to recruit its own officials, which meant that the bureaucracy turned over at each change of government. One expert on the subject calculated that 99 percent of public recruitment before World War II was "politically" motivated.[28]

From 1943 to 1955, the functions of the state were dramatically increased through nationalizations and the expansion of the government's role in foreign and domestic trade, the banking system, and industrial promotion. In addition, the number of public employees in the central government increased by almost 150 percent. Even though regulations for modernizing and professionalizing governmental organization were written, politicization and the practice of patronage continued and, in some cases, worsened.[29] The administrations of this period drastically increased the size and functions of the government without possessing the technical and administrative capabilities necessary to carry out efficiently and adequately the tasks involved (there was no school in the country for training public officials).

The Argentine government was unable to create bureaucratic enclaves of excellence as Brazil had done in its National Development Bank, the Ministry of Foreign Affairs, and the Getulio Vargas Foundation, and as Mexico had done in the Treasury Department and the Bank of Mexico, and with Nacional Financiera (NAFINSA), where well-paid, trained officials loyal to the state were promoted on the basis of merit and were relatively isolated from corporate interests, politicization, and cronyism. These officials were technically and administratively capable of carrying out fairly rational policies and had an esprit de corps strong enough to enable them to curb the most flagrant excesses of the ruling class and corporate interests. Brazil reorganized its public institutions on the North American model in the mid-1930s, during the administration of President Getulio Vargas. The concept that one should enter public service through entrance exams and that different salaries should be given to career and appointed officials was introduced.[30] Only at the end of the 1950s, twenty years later, did a similar process begin in Argentina. In Mexico, access to the highest political positions has been reserved for members of a highly professionalized bureaucratic/political structure. Study at the Autonomous University of Mexico, graduate study in the United States, and a career in the Treasury Department, Ministry of Planning, or NAFINSA were the indispensable requisites for reaching a high position in the administration of the economy and, in recent decades, for holding the highest office in the land, as exemplified by presidents Miguel de la Madrid and Carlos Salinas de Gortari.[31]

In Argentina, the discrepancy between assigned responsibilities and the capacity to execute policy was very great. This is probably one of the relevant factors behind the substantial differences between the performance of Argentina's economy and Brazil's and Mexico's in recent decades. In 1989, Argentina's per capita GDP was only slightly higher than Brazil's and Mexico's, but it had been respectively four and two times higher in 1938. All three nations implemented relatively similar growth strategies (development from within) during the postwar period, obtaining very different results. While Argentina's economy stagnated, Brazil's and Mexico's economies converged toward the average standard of living and levels of productivity in Argentina. The explanation for this divergence is too complex to examine in depth here, but it is obvious that significant differences in the quality and organizational capacity of the respective governments played a major role. Although government organizations in Brazil and Mexico are far from being models of efficiency and professionalism, both countries ran their governmental apparatus more efficiently than Argentina.

Another reason for institutional differences between Argentina, Japan, and South Korea was that in Argentina sectoral and corporatist interests (business groups, unions, professional organizations, regional interests, and the armed forces, to name just a few) have traditionally been very strong. With the military coup d'état in 1930, the consolidation of corporatist interests began, a process that accelerated significantly under the postwar civilian and military governments. Ministers representing these interests have been more the rule than the exception. The control of key positions by sectoral interests that, in theory, should be regulated and promoted by government institutions, is common in Argentina. The concept of conflict of interest in public service is practically unknown, nor is there much awareness of its significance among the general public.

Given the corporate institutional framework in which vast segments of the Argentine ruling class have operated, it is no surprise that the policies of the interventionist state rarely had a pro-competition or pro-market character in Argentina as they did in Japan and South Korea. To illustrate this point, we need only remember how, under the pressure of sectoral and regional interests, the Argentine government subsidized economic sectors in decline (sugar, cotton, and yerba mate tea), nationalized bankrupt companies (Giol, Austral, and Siam), saved private companies from bankruptcy (particularly those excessively indebted in dollars that survived thanks to foreign-exchange risk insurance guaranteed by successive governments between 1981 and 1985), sustained unproductive and structurally deficient industries for years (the state iron ore mining and coal industries), and promoted, through costly subsidies, activities that at the time seemed "highly advanced" (atomic energy), whose economic results ultimately proved disappointing.

In addition, many of the regulations introduced by successive governments during the period reduced competition, blocked more efficient resource allocation, and avoided or retarded the necessary and painful productive conversion inherent in all economic growth. The combination of strong corporatist groups and an organizationally weak government that was attempting to implement strong interventionist economic and social policies produced results totally at odds with the objectives of economic growth and national independence that generated the interventions in the first place.

If Argentina had had a strong and well-organized government and flexible sectoral interests and had chosen appropriate economic and social policies, state intervention to promote development or social justice might have been successful, at least for a while. Regrettably, this was not the reality, and the creation and strengthening of the interventionist state not only seriously distorted the workings of the markets, but also gradually crippled the foundation of the state itself. Militarism, populism, and a deep-rooted inability to develop a stable and democratic political system created a defective institutional framework unable to facilitate modernization.

In short, from 1940 to 1973, Argentina was moving against the tide of history, regularly enforcing policies contrary to those of the nations that grew after the war. Among those nations ranked as advanced in 1938, Argentina was the one with the poorest economic performance after 1940, and, in relative terms, it fell behind not only economically, but politically and institutionally as well.

STAGNATION AND THE CRISIS OF THE INTERVENTIONIST STATE (1973–1990)

From a political standpoint, these trends were aggravated during the period between 1973 and 1983. The democratically elected Peronist government of 1973–1976 faltered as a result of the violence generated by a strong and growing guerrilla movement, ineffective populist economic policies, and deep conflicts between the right (nationalist) and left (socialist/Marxist) wings of the Peronist party. The military government that replaced it initiated a major reform of the economy that it was unable to complete. It also engaged in repressive policies against the guerrilla movement and its allies, policies that were perceived, both in Argentina and abroad, as violating basic human rights. Finally, it launched the ill-fated Malvinas invasion in 1982. Military defeat accelerated the transfer of power to a civilian government in 1983.

From an economic standpoint, by 1973 the adverse consequences of the government's economic policies and the unrelenting growth of the interventionist state had begun to weigh heavily. Annual average growth of per capita GDP stood at 0.9 percent in the 1970s and fell to a negative 2.5 percent in the 1980s. Argentina's rank, based on per capita GDP, fell from nineteenth place in 1965, to twenty-sixth in 1989 (see table 3). The economic crisis was aggravated in the 1970s and 1980s by a high fiscal deficit by international standards (the average annual fiscal deficit for the public sector was approximately

8.3 percent between 1973 and 1990) and galloping inflation (annual average inflation reached 152 percent between 1973 and 1984, and 382 percent between 1984 and
1988). Argentina was one of the few countries in which
per capita income dwindled (it fell 26 percent between
1973 and 1990) and income distribution deteriorated.[32]
Although there were great fluctuations in the rate of
inflation during this period, overall it was so high that it is
accurate to say that the country endured in a permanent
"regime of high inflation."[33] As a result of this inflation
and general economic instability, the economy gradually
demonetized and the money supply, defined as M3 (currency, deposit accounts, savings accounts, and fixed-
term deposits), fell gradually but dramatically from
nearly 27.1 percent of GDP in 1970, to an average of 16.6
percent in the period from 1982 to 1988, reaching a low
of 5.7 percent in the middle of the hyperinflation crisis
of 1990.

With the worsening of the crisis in the 1980s, tax
revenues as a percentage of GDP began to fall, and the
relative share of taxes that negatively distorted the allocation of resources (taxes on bank debits, fuels, exports, and assets) grew. With tax revenues falling, the
inflation tax (which results from the printing of money by
the government) began to grow, representing, on average, 6.5 percent of GDP for this period. Consolidated
public spending (federal, provincial, and municipal public enterprises and retirement benefits) grew from approximately 39 percent of GDP in 1970, to 56 percent in
the 1980–88 period. There were nearly 2,250,000 public
employees in federal, provincial, and municipal governments and government-owned firms and banks in 1989,
representing approximately 19 percent of the economically active population.

TABLE 7. ECONOMIC PERFORMANCE INDICATORS (1973–1990)

	1973/76	1977/79	1980/83	1984/88	1989/90
GDP Growth (annual avg. %)	2.1	2.2	-1.8	0.5	-3.1[a]
Population (millions end of period)	26.5	27.7	29.6	32.0	32.9
Per Capita (GDP growth %)	0.4	0.6	-3.5	-0.8	-4.4[a]
Investment/GDP (%)	22.3	22.9	22.4	18.3[c]	15.0[a]
Unemployment (%)	4.1	2.7	5.2	5.9	6.7
Consumer Prices Inflation (annual avg. %)	108.9	170.3	178.5	382.6	1086.6
M3/GDP (%)	28.3	30.5	21.8	18.5	9.0
Public Expenditure/GDP (annual avg.%)	44.2[b]	45.6[b]	54.7[b]	57.4[b]	50.7
Fiscal Deficit/GDP	9.3[b]	3.4[b]	9.7[b]	8.4[b]	9.1
Openness Coefficient	8.5	10.3	8.4	6.6	5.5

Sources: Banco Central de la República Argentina: *Cuentas Nacionales* (1976,1994) and *Boletín Estadístico* (1960–1994); Instituto Nacional de Estadísticas y Censos, *Informes sobre el Comercio Exterior argentino* (1973–1994); Fundación de Investigaciones Económicas Latinoamericanas: *El Gasto Público en la Argentina, 1960-1988* (Buenos Aires: FIEL 1990), and *Indicadores de Coyuntura* (1973–1994); Ministerio de Economía, Secretaría de Programacion Económica (1992).

[a] Banco Central de la República Argentina, *Cuentas Nacionales 1980-1993* (April 1993).

[b] Fundacion de Investigaciones Económicas Latinoamericanas, *El Gasto Público en la Argentina, 1960-1988* (1990); expenditures include federal, provincial, and municipal government enterprises and health and retirement benefits. The central bank's deficit (quasi-fiscal) is not included.

Argentina also lived with large and growing deficits. The annual average deficit of the public sector, consolidated from 1973 to 1980, was about 6.4 percent of GDP, and it grew steadily during the next decade, when the annual average reached 9.1 percent. If the deficit of the central bank (generated by subsidies on interest rates, multiple exchange rates, forward foreign-exchange risk insurance contracts, and defaulted credits) is added in, the public-sector deficit for the 1980s would average approximately 11 percent of GDP. The deficits were the result of increased public spending for populist policies, such as new welfare programs and substantial increases in wages of government employees (1973 to 1976), increases in public investment in infrastructure and arms purchases (1977 to 1982), massive increases in public employment at the provincial level (1983 to 1989), and the increased costs associated with a general deterioration of the government's ability to carry out its administrative functions.

In Argentina's mixed economy the private sector generated about 70 percent of GDP and the public sector generated the other 30 percent. But the role of the public sector in the economy was much larger than these numbers indicate because the private sector was highly regulated. Furthermore, the public sector expenditures from 1973 to 1988 averaged 51 percent of GDP (including public health, pensions, social assistance, and subsidies and transfers to the business sector).

The accumulation of significant foreign debt from 1977 to 1983 also weakened the fiscal performance of the public sector. As of December 31, 1983, Argentina's foreign debt was approximately $45 billion. Through various procedures (especially forward foreign-exchange risk insurance contracts), a large part of the debt (approximately $13 billion) was transferred from the private sector to the public sector between 1981 and 1985.[34] The strong surge of international interest rates starting in 1980, a significant increase of the stock of public debt, and the simultaneous closing of international financial sources combined to produce the so-called foreign debt crisis. This crisis contributed significantly to the public sector's fiscal deterioration due to heavy debt-service payments, increased economic uncertainty, and capital flight motivated by the fear of fiscal collapse.

Between 1973 and 1989, the Argentine government's ability to collect funds and finance its growing deficits declined. The social security system, which enjoyed a surplus in the 1970s, went into deficit in the next decade; access to international credit was lost at the start of the debt crisis in 1982; the tax system gradually lost the ability to collect taxes to keep pace with the rate of inflation; and the inflation tax fell, together with the demand for money and the rapid demonetization of the economy.

This general deterioration in Argentina's economic performance occurred simultaneously with a rapid deterioration of the economy's institutional framework. The intensity and frequency of government intervention in areas as varied as salaries, interest rates, taxes, and exchange controls escalated tremendously. Between 1973 and 1990, there were thirteen years of exchange controls and sixteen years of general price controls. The government was an active and disorderly participant in industrial development through subsidized credits, guarantees to the private sector, fiscal deferments, and a broad array of other government support programs. It created programs to promote industrial exports and regional development. The government participated in the detailed regulation and promotion of activities as diverse as transportation, insurance, mining, fishing, petroleum, steel, navigational services, and wholesale and retail business.

The rise of government discretionary action (unexpected foreign exchange and price controls, devaluations, permanent changes in taxation rules, etc.), the severe political conflicts that characterized the 1973–1983 period, and the serious deterioration in the ability of the judicial system to resolve business disputes increased levels of uncertainty and exacerbated the crisis in two ways. First, government discretionary action and its counterpart, economic uncertainty, reduced the size and efficiency of the markets.[35] Permanent changes in the rules of the game encouraged economic agents to withdraw from formal markets. Off-the-books employment, capital flight, the growth of the informal economy, and the emigration of skilled workers were common during the 1970s and 1980s (it is unofficially estimated that nearly 600,000 people emigrated between 1970 and 1990). Such behavior reflected the defensive reaction of large segments of the population to the serious distortions of the rules of the game and the growing discretionary action of successive governments in both the economic and social spheres. Second, discretionary government actions significantly raised the risks for private investors. At first, they distorted investment flows, as investors moved toward protected and subsidized areas, and stimulated the undertaking of projects with low profitability and a quick turnover in terms of the economy as a whole. Later, absolute levels of private investment fell, and financial speculation and capital flight became the norm.[36]

By 1983, as a result of the foreign debt crisis, investments were restricted by the extremely high rates of return investors required in order to compensate for the increasing risk of government insolvency. Gross investment declined dramatically from an annual average level of 22.5 percent of GDP between 1973 and 1983, to approximately 16.7 percent between 1984 and 1990, an inadequate level to sustain economic growth (see table 7). Since public-sector investment declined less than private-sector investment in the 1980s, it ended up accounting for 40 percent of total gross investment, a fairly high number for a private-sector-driven capitalist economy.

Among the most curious phenomena of this period were the high overall investment levels (see table 2 in the appendix) and low growth rates that characterized Argentina's economy from 1970 to 1983. This low investment productivity can be explained chiefly by Argentina's isolation from the international economy, the low level of competition in the domestic economy, excessive interventionism, and acute political instability. Argentina's average openness coefficient was 9 percent between 1973 and 1983, and 6 percent between 1984 and 1990. In essence, the strategy of development from within produced serious distortions in the economy's relative prices, which led to poor resource allocation and reduced productivity of investment flows in the private sector.[37] Import-substitution policies were expanded in the 1970s. With strong state support, the private sector broadened its participation in the industrialization process to include intermediate industrial products (namely petrochemicals, paper, steel, cement, and aluminum). Despite an active promotional policy for industrial exports, the main objective of which was to compensate through strong fiscal and financial incentives for the anti-export bias of its development-from-within strategy, Argentina was unable to generate a significant and sustained flow of industrial exports. Between 1973 and

1991, exports of industrial manufactures increased in real terms at an average rate of only 2.3 percent, despite heavy promotional subsidies estimated to represent between 25 and 35 percent of the value of exported goods.[38] Furthermore, a substantial portion of these industrial commodities exports was from capital-intensive sectors with high fixed costs (steel, aluminum, petrochemicals) that preferred to export and at least recover their variable costs rather than to reduce their levels of production and the rate of utilitization of their installed capacity. Argentina was faced with highly competitive international markets, in which national supply was marginal and the country was a price taker, which contributed to the deterioration in the terms of trade that adversely affected Argentina's economy during the 1980s (see table 5 in the appendix). Once the opportunities to extend the process of import substitution were exhausted, and efforts to create an industrial sector with a large export capability had failed, industrial activity stagnated and the sector could no longer create new jobs. Annual growth rates during the 1970s (2.2 percent) and the 1980s (– 1.8 percent) were substantially lower than in preceding decades.[39]

The second factor inhibiting Argentina's investment productivity was the low level of competition, which adversely affected private-sector investment. The causes of this low level of competition were excessive government regulation, intense economic concentration resulting from oligopolistic and monopolistic market structures, the growth of the monopolistic public sector, and the increasing isolation of the domestic economy from international competition. These interrelated phenomena reduced the effectiveness of market mechanisms for allocating resources and distributing income among production factors. In the tradeable-goods sector, the domestic supply of a broad array of final and intermediate products was dominated by a small group of enterprises. This would not have been worrisome had the economy been exposed to international markets, which could have curbed oligopolistic price-fixing tendencies. In addition, Argentina's economy was characterized by uncompetitive markets in the service sector and in wholesale trade, transportation, the liberal professions, and the labor markets, where the concentration of supply, regulated prices, and competition restrictions were the rule. Such severe restrictions on competition in a relatively small national economic framework (Argentina's estimated GDP for 1991 was approximately three times smaller than Brazil's, six times smaller than Italy's, and thirty times smaller than that of the United States) seriously limited economies of scale and specialization. Dwindling competition reduced pressures for innovation and absorption of new technologies, impeded resource allocation to the most productive sectors, and created an economic environment in which the business class gained more by obtaining privileges and "quasi-rents" from the government than by creating new products, discovering new markets, or improving management and production methods.

The third factor contributing to Argentina's low investment productivity was the increasingly ineffectual and often disruptive intervention of the government in economic life. Argentina's historically weak government did not develop the organizational capabilities necessary to discharge the growing responsibilities and functions it sought to fulfill, however, and the failure of the interventionist state had perverse effects on economic performance. Investment productivity for public-sector enterprises was historically very low. Overemployment, investment cost overruns, mistakes in resource allocation, and huge operating costs were evidence of the low productivity and poor management of public-sector resources. In addition, the overall efficiency of public spending was very low at both the federal and provincial levels. Several independent studies by the Fundación de Investigaciones Económicas Latinoamericanas (FIEL), the Comision Económica para América Latina (CEPAL), and the Fundación Mediterranea on the quality and efficiency of public spending have confirmed the serious managerial deficiencies in the administration of the public sector. Overall public opinion as reflected in surveys is that government provision of goods and services is poor, levels of quality and management are low, and corruption is excessively high.

Finally, an array of circular and cumulative political effects generated by economic decline contributed to low investment productivity. Stagnation aggravated latent social and political conflicts in the society and contributed to a period of intense political instability (1960–1983) during which fourteen presidents alternated in power and the composition of the Supreme Court was changed on five occasions.

The growth of public spending, uncontrolled fiscal policies, and rampant inflation were not only the causes, but also the consequences, of a defective and perverse relationship between the government and civil society and between the world of politics and the world of special interests. Argentina developed an economic regime in which the function of allocating resources and distributing income to production factors took place, not through market mechanisms or government budgets, but through a system dominated by relentless, uncaring pressure groups and institutionalized corruption, in which the ruling elite frequently preferred populist demagoguery or antidemocratic authoritarianism to rational policies that would have required confronting and winning the electorate with somewhat more realistic and honest choices and policies.

The government's weakness and instability, and the excessive politicization of economic policy, resulted in the poor allocation of economic resources, in both the public and private sectors, hindering the country's growth potential. This process, in turn, aggravated social conflict, particularly between the urban and rural sectors of the society, pitting those who generated most of their income from transfers and government spending against those dependent on private-sector consumption and investment. Political instability, military coups, and populist politics, as well as periodic and, over time, escalating violence in the country's political life, weakened the tottering institutional framework and deepened the society's woes. The savage conflicts between opposing social and political groups were the primary cause of political instability and led to drastic changes in economic policy. As the struggle for power and revenue intensified, the sinecure state (in which opposing interests fought over the distribution of privileges and sinecures) was the final ironic and painful end of the interventionist state. Having been picked clean by one interest group after another, the government gradually lost its authority. Finally, after exhausting all its financial resources, it went bankrupt in 1989.

What is most surprising about Argentina's case is the extremes to which the government went to enact a vision that was isolationist, statist, and hostile to the workings of the international system when it was perfectly obvious that the countries that were making progress were implementing diametrically opposite policies. But even as Argentina's economic crisis was worsening, sectors of Argentina's ruling elite continued to prosper through their exercise of power, speculation, and access to the privileges granted by a state that, to all appearances, dominated the economic life of the country but, in reality, had simply become the instrument for redistributing income from the many to the few.

The long period of economic decline which began in the early 1970s has produced considerable economic hardship for the Argentine people. Real wages per worker fell between 20 and 30 percent between 1980 and 1990 (see table 4 in appendix), with the sharpest decline occurring during the hyperinflation period of 1989–1990. Also in the 1980s the adjustment policies pursued to generate a surplus in the trade balance relied heavily on nominal devaluations of the domestic currency, further depressing real earned wages.

This process was aggravated during the 1980s as a result of the serious deterioration of the government apparatus (particularly in the areas of public health, public education, security, and public services). Indirect indicators of social welfare (for example, years of schooling, access to water and sewage) all point toward a deterioration in the living standards and in the overall distribution of income during the 1980s. The consequences of the crisis were not borne equally by all social groups. The wealthy could usually protect their wealth by transfering their assets abroad. Those without substantial savings did not enjoy an equivalent escape mechanism.

Although real wages during the 1980s declined significantly, total household income probably fell by a lesser amount since it seems that individual members of households began to work more hours in the same job and more members of households joined the work force.

The hyperinflation crises of 1989 and early 1990 brought home the pressing need to resolve the problem of the fiscal deficit. Hyperinflation was the final result of a long, slow process of "dollarization" of savings and capital flight, which ended up shutting off all the government's sources of financing. The crisis reached its climax with the financial collapse of the government, which followed the confiscation of individual deposits (December 1989), the repeated compulsory refinancing of the public debt (1983–1992), and the hyperinflations of 1989 and 1990. The creators of the interventionist state never dreamed that their economic policies would end up devouring the very state they had meant to strengthen.

•

Argentina's experience clearly shows the importance of the relationship between the availability of production factors, technological innovation, market size, and the quality of economic organization. The low growth of Argentina's economy during the postwar period was not the result of the lack of production factors—the country is rich in raw materials and land and has a growing and skilled labor force. Until the beginning of the foreign debt crisis in 1982, the country maintained a relatively high level of savings and physical investment (average gross fixed investment for the 1960–1982 period was 21.5 percent of GDP). Nevertheless, despite high levels of investment in fixed assets and the society's large annual expenditures on education (about 5 percent of GDP), growth rates were relatively modest and compared unfavorably with those of nations with similar or lower rates of investment in fixed assets, including Denmark, the United States, Italy, Mexico, New Zealand, and Sweden, or countries with less-skilled human resources, such as South Korea, Hong Kong, Singapore, Taiwan, Mexico, and Brazil.[40]

Although its national market is small, Argentina's postwar economy has been one of the most closed in the world. Its total annual average foreign trade in real goods and services for the years 1986–1988 was approximately $16.9 billion, representing about 6.1 percent of GDP and leaving Argentina in one hundred and seventeenth place among 126 nations. (Only Bangladesh, Brazil, Burma, the Dominican Republic, Sudan, Iran, Iraq, India, and the USSR ranked lower.)[41] Yet Argentina not only has kept itself isolated from international trade flows, losing opportunities to increase the size of its market and take advantage of economies of scale and specialization, but its internal economic organization has also been extremely inadequate. The deterioration of Argentina's economic organization served not only to distort resource allocation and reduce efficiency in the economy, but, over time, reduced the rate of capital accumulation and condemned the economy to stagnation and decline.

The adoption of an interventionist strategy led to the overextension of the state in economic and regulatory activities. This adversely affected the state's operations in general, seriously distorted the functioning of the markets, and indisputably prejudiced the country's economic performance. Beginning in the 1970s, political instability and social conflict aggravated the major flaws of economic organization. Combined with extravagant fiscal and monetary policies that produced extreme volatility in the macroeconomic environment (immense fiscal deficits, expansive and uncontrolled monetary policies), this instability produced a high-inflation regime and a growing uncertainty that slowly but surely reduced the rates of accumulation of physical and human capital and brought the country to the most severe economic crisis in its history.[42]

It is on the basis of this blunt but realistic diagnosis of the underlying causes of Argentina's economic and institutional decay that we can specify the fundamental objectives that must guide Argentina in the future, if it wishes to establish a new economic and institutional regime that will, through a process of convergence, permit it to rejoin, in the space of a generation, the group of most advanced nations:

- stabilization of the economy and the reduction of inflation to international levels, especially through monetary reform and control of the fiscal deficit;
- reestablishment of market operations as the essential mechanism for resource allocation and the distribution of production factors;
- reform of the government at the national and provincial levels and the curbing of its economic role through a major program of privatization of public enterprises and sale of other assets, an active policy of deregulation, the elimination of public largesse in the distribution of appointments, early retirement for public employees, sweeping fiscal reform, and spending cuts;
- creation of a strong state apparatus, based on administrative competence in executing those functions that cannot be delegated to the private sector and able to exercise its regulatory functions effectively while resisting the pressures of corporatist interests;
- reintegration of the country's economy into the international economy by opening the domestic market to competing imports, and simultaneously generating a strong flow of exports with high value added, by attracting foreign capital and human resources, and by accelerating the incorporation of available advanced technologies into the domestic economy;

- improving the income distribution structure, encouraging greater social mobility to allow the majority of the population, despite social frictions and dislocations, to fully participate in the benefits resulting from economic growth;
- developing and strengthening an independent and effective legal and judicial system to settle disputes between private parties and protect the private sector from the discretionary actions of the government.

Before assessing Argentina's prospects for the future, however, we must first examine the steps it has taken toward reform.

Chapter 3

ECONOMIC AND STRUCTURAL REFORM FROM 1989 TO 1994

The origins of the economic reform initiated in 1989 are to be found in the mounting crisis that had afflicted Argentine society since the mid-1970s. Economic stagnation, the regime of high inflation, the collapse of the interventionist state, and the resulting political instability made society aware that the economic system had to be changed. Although a consensus about the need for thoroughgoing reform of the economy began to form in the early 1980s, no prescription for how to achieve this end was put forward. Harsh criticism of the status quo and a clamor for reform were accompanied by piecemeal proposals tailored to the interests of the proposers. Change was indeed necessary, but it should come at someone else's expense.

The combination of the failure of the last military government, Argentina's defeat in the Malvinas war, and the worsening state of the economy had a cathartic effect on the country, however. Opinion polls indicated, as early as 1983, deep and positive shifts in public opinion on subjects as varied as the role of private economic activity and the state in society, and the integration of Argentina into the world economy. The rejection of corporatist power groups and support for democracy were becoming apparent. A strong desire to emulate the political and economic models prevalent in the great industrial democracies of the postwar period could also be clearly observed.

The crisis gave way to malaise, impatience, and, through a painful series of ups and downs, a social awareness of the outlines of a new economic regime. Reform got under way in fits and starts, but the process really began in 1983, with the reestablishment of a democratic political system, which enjoyed massive popular support. The system was reinforced by the legitimate transfer of political power from President Raul Alfonsín to Carlos Saúl Menem in July 1989. (The last time a democratically elected government had replaced a democratically elected government of a different party was in 1916.)

It is probable that the severity of the economic situation in Argentina would have led to sweeping economic reform with or without democratic institutions, as in South Korea (1962), Brazil (1964), and Chile (1975). It is the combination of the reestablishment of democracy in 1983, the beginning of the first serious attempt at economic reform with the Austral Plan in 1985, the difficult but successful political transition of July 1989, and the beginning of in-depth economic reform in 1989–1990 that makes Argentina's experience unique.

Serious economic reform, within the framework of a fully operating democracy, requires a broad political and social consensus. The resulting new economic regime can then be legitimized and strengthened through debate, trial and error, and the changes in political power that characterize democratic governments. Although it is true that such countries as Chile, South Korea, Brazil, and Mexico were able to modernize their economic structures and speed their growth in an authoritarian or, at best, barely democratic institutional framework, it is no accident that democracy is the dominant political system in the world's twenty most advanced countries. During the initial phases of economic modernization or after a national catastrophe, an authoritarian but stable political system may have greater means at its disposal than a nonconsolidated democratic regime for introducing the economic, political, and social reforms necessary to initiate rapid growth. Nevertheless, once the process of investment and growth takes hold, the entrepreneurial liberties that characterize a strong private sector generating employment and wealth inevitably begin to seek expression in political liberties. Furthermore, given a certain level of social and cultural development, the democratic system has demonstrated its superiority in carrying out the complex social and political engineering that sustained growth requires. There is ample historical evidence that democratic governments provide a more flexible institutional framework for the negotiated settlement of the conflicts and tensions that economic growth unfailingly produces.

From 1983 onward, public opinion polls in Argentina revealed a growing concern over inflation, low salaries, and economic instability. By mid-decade, this concern extended to the deterioration of public services, education, health care, and security, and to government corruption. This swing in public opinion profoundly affected the rules of the political game, as can be seen from the results of the legislative elections of 1985, 1987, 1991, and 1993, and from the presidential election of 1989, when the electorate judged candidates on their economic stewardship in office. Concrete issues related to stability and the quality of life gained ascendancy over the usual ideological disputes and demagogic promises that had previously characterized postwar Argentine politics. As a result, the traditional political parties began to put forth candidates with untraditional profiles, including businessmen, journalists, academics, artists, and famous athletes.

Beginning in 1983, independent research institutes, among them the Centro de Estudios de Estado y Sociedad (CEDES), the Centro de Estudios Monetarios Argentinos (CEMA), FIEL, the Fundación Mediterranea, the Instituto de Desarrollo Económico y Social (IDES), and the Di Tella Institute, and international organizations such as the World Bank, the IMF, the Japanese-government-sponsored Okita Report, and CEPAL, assumed an important role in addressing the crisis.

To varying degrees, these organizations helped put Argentina's problems in perspective, provided empirical data and international comparisons, gave focus to the debate, and afforded a greater depth to policy analysis. Despite disagreements over specific policies, reflecting the different schools of economic thought and political positions and interests, historians in the future will no doubt identify the appearance of a zeitgeist characterized by strong criticism of the status quo and a shared interest in establishing a new economic regime.

The reform of Argentina's economy began in 1985 with the Austral Plan (the austral was the new currency), which clearly defined for the first time the paradigm of the economic regime to be sought: economic stability and fiscal reform (as a precondition for growth), structural governmental reform (characterized by the cutting of subsidies, an independent central bank, deregulation, and privatizations), economic liberalization (with the gradual dismantling of protectionist policies and a stable exchange rate), and a consensual renegotiation of the external debt with foreign creditors. Unfortunately, the initial success of the plan gave way to failure, the academic discussion of which has been extensive. The plan's failure has been blamed on, among other things, its heterodox characteristics,[1] the inertia of the inflationary process (with its cycles of stabilization, resurgence, new controls, and new plans), a chronic fiscal deficit, and the institutional and political instability that accelerated the replacement of assets denominated in the domestic currency by foreign currency assets, provoking "attacks of speculation" against central bank reserves in 1989.[2]

The most important reason for failure was, in my opinion, the inability of President Alfonsín's government to carry out the painful fiscal and structural adjustments needed to establish stability. The government either did not think it was strong enough or lacked the conviction to overcome the iron opposition of various groups blocking change. Among these groups were the unions of government employees, fearful of losing their jobs, whose ruling elites often participated in the control of government-owned enterprises; business sectors that benefited from government subsidies or inflated sales to the public sector, or who made money from minimally productive businesses that could only have survived in the shelter of strong protectionist and interventionist policies; corrupt officials who got rich from the system; segments of the ruling class unwilling to forgo their discretionary prerogatives over public expenditures; and speculators who profited from a setting of acute economic instability and volatility. Perhaps the main contribution of the plan was that it showed the community the advantages of living with stability and the importance of fiscal and structural reforms to the success of stabilization policies.

The country had to wait four more years, however—until hyperinflation, which encouraged the introduction of changes that would not otherwise easily gain support, and the collapse of the state provided the necessary impetus—to see the beginning of such reforms. Undoubtedly, it was the hyperinflation crisis of 1989 and early 1990 that overcame the resistance of the special interest groups.

ECONOMIC REFORM FROM JULY 1989 TO SEPTEMBER 1994

The economic reform program undertaken by the Menem administration, which took office in July 1989, can be divided into three different but sequential phases.

July–December 1989

During the first phase, the management of the economy was placed in the hands of a team from the Bunge and Born Group, one of the most important business groups in the country. President Menem's selection represented a major break with the anti-big-business Peronist tradition. The so-called "BB" Plan called for a "heterodox" effort to stabilize the economy, control inflation, and improve fiscal accounts. Adjustments, and then freezes, of variables controlled by the government (such as the exchange rate, tariffs, public utilities service rates, and government employees' salaries) and a price agreement with the private sector were implemented. Payments to public-sector suppliers and contractors were frozen, and domestic government debt began to be refinanced on a longer-term basis.

Simultaneously, two key laws were enacted by the National Congress (with opposition support) to bring about structural reforms and restore fiscal solvency. The Economic Emergency Law suspended (initially for a term of 180 days and subsequently extended periodically up to the present) almost all subsidies to the private

TABLE 8. ECONOMIC PERFORMANCE INDICATORS

	1989	1990	1991	1992	1993
GDP Growth[a] (annual avg. %)	−6.2	0.1	8.9	8.7	6.0[d]
Population (in millions)	32.3	32.8	33.3	33.7	34.1[d]
GDP Growth[a] (% per capita)	−7.5	−1.4	7.4	7.2	4.5[a]
Gross Investment/ GDP %[a]	15.7	14.2	16.3	19.6	21.0[d]
Unemployment (%)	7.1	6.3	6.4	6.9	9.6[d]
CPI Inflation	3079.0	2314.0	84.0	17.5	6.6
Wholesale Inflation %	3432.0	1606.0	56.7	3.2	−0.8
M3/GDP (%)	12.2	5.7	6.5	9.6	12.1[d]
Public Expenditures[b]/GDP %	25.9	26.6	27.0	27.2	27.6
Consolidated Deficit[c]/GDP %	−13.7	−2.3	−1.3	−0.4	−1.0[c]
Openness Coefficient	5.0	5.9	6.3	7.4	7.5[d]
International Reserves (year's end)	2928.6	6010.1	8974.4	12495.8	17393.0[d]

Sources: Banco Central de la República Argentina: *Cuentas Nacionales* (1976, 1994) and *Boletín Estadístico* (1960–1994); Instituto Nacional de Estadísticas y Censos, *Informes sobre el Comercio Exterior Argentino* (1973–1994); Fundación Investigaciones Economicas Latinoamericanas: *El Gasto Público en la Argentina*, 1960–1988 (Buenos Aires: FIEL 1990), and *Indicadores de Coyuntura* (1973–1994); Ministerio de Economía, Secretaría de Programación Económica (1994).

[a] BCRA, April 1993.
[b] Ministerio de Economía, Secretaría de Programacion Económica. Includes national, provincial and municipal administrations, plus the net financing needs of government enterprises, the social security system (excluding health benefits) and family assistance programs.
[c] Does not include the central bank's fiscal deficit.
[d] Preliminary estimates.

sector then in effect, as well as all extraordinary government expenditures (e.g., industrial-promotion arrangements, regional subsidies, export subsidies, and lawsuits against the government). The Government Reform Law set up the regulatory framework for the transfer of firms and assets from the public to the private sector.

Inflation, as measured by the consumer price index, fell precipitously from 197 percent in July 1989 (the first month of hyperinflation) to 9.4 percent, 5.6 percent, and 6.5 percent in September, October, and November 1989, respectively. But the honeymoon was soon over and, by December, the stabilization plan had derailed. Doubts about the sustainability of the fixed exchange rate had surfaced, which caused the government to institute a steep preemptive 50 percent devaluation of the currency, which in turn triggered a run on the currency and a burst of inflation (the consumer price index hit 40 percent in December). But, in reality, the plan failed because the measures taken were sufficient neither to allay the stark lack of confidence that reined in the country nor to satisfy the demand of economic agents for a severe fiscal adjustment and a swift implementation of structural reforms.

December 1989–January 1991

The second phase of economic reform corresponded to the tenure in office of Economic Minister Erman González. The new minister was a close associate of President Menem and had in the past held the position of minister of finance of the province of La Rioja during Menem's tenure as governor. The new economic team that surrounded him decided on total liberation of the currency exchange market, abolished all price controls, and confronted the serious quasi-fiscal deficit that had resulted from the domestic public debt by instituting a long-term rescheduling of that debt. From the government's viewpoint, the domestic public debt (measured in terms of government securities and reserve requirements in the financial sector) had reached unmanageable levels, in addition to being almost entirely indexed to the inflation rate or to the dollar, which made it impossible to reduce through inflation. During the last quarter of 1989, the central bank fiscal deficit accounted for almost 5 percent of GDP, and monthly interest payments for almost 50 percent of the monetary base.

To correct this situation, at the end of December the government compulsorily refinanced the term deposits of the banking sector and the remaining short-term public debt through exchange of a ten-year bond in dollars, the 1989 BONEX. This measure, while necessary, caused a great loss of confidence because of its negative impact on property rights and produced a second wave of hyperinflation. The monthly inflation index jumped to 79.2 percent, 61.6 percent, and 95.6 percent for January, February, and March 1990, respectively. Interestingly, during the period that followed, the economy stabilized with floating exchange rates. Average monthly inflation from April through December held at 11 percent.

From the standpoint of reform, 1990 was a key political year. Beginning in March, the authorities began to put the Economic Emergency Law into practice. Financing of the Treasury by the central bank was prohibited, and the management of several government banks, including the Banco Hipotecario Nacional and the Banco Nacional Desarrollo, was changed. To balance fiscal accounts, payments to public contractors and solicitation of new public contract bids were suspended, public-sector collective bargaining agreements were repudiated, and payments to firms benefiting from state-sponsored industrial promotion schemes were deferred.

With regard to monetary policy, various factors that had stimulated the printing of money were eliminated: through credit mechanisms, subsidies, and differential payments schemes the central bank had become an agent financing and supporting (on behalf of government-owned national and provincial banks) nontraditional exports, the welfare and social security systems, and assorted regional, sectoral, and corporate interests. Another interesting aspect of monetary policy was that over the course of the year the central bank accumulated international reserves in excess of $3 billion; these reserves were bought against pesos issued by the central bank to satisfy the demand for peso remonetization and later provided the resources for implementing the program of convertibility in April 1991.

Certain in-depth structural reforms were also initiated during this period. With respect to trade liberalization, the maximum tariff was brought down to 24 percent from 30 percent, the tariffs dispersion[3] was reduced, and specific fees and quantitative restrictions were eliminated. With respect to deregulation, advances were made in the oil, ports, and transportation sectors. The national telephone company (ENTEL) and Aerolíneas Argentinas were privatized, as were other minor enterprises.

Despite these instances of progress, public finances deteriorated further in the final months of 1990, the result of provincial financial deficits (which had serious repercussions for the official provincial banks) and the severe deficits of the social security system. Income from privatizations postponed the encroaching crisis for a time, but the fiscal frailty of the government's operating accounts and an increase of political uncertainty spurred a sharp rise in interest rates and a run on the dollar. An attempt to stabilize the exchange rate through sales of reserves by the central bank was not sufficient to reestablish confidence, and inflation again began to increase and depreciation of the local currency began to accelerate.

January 1991–October 1994

The third phase of economic reform began in January 1991, when President Menem appointed Domingo Cavallo, formerly minister of foreign relations, as minister of the economy. Cavallo aimed to reestablish confidence and stability by setting a fixed rate of exchange for the currency convertible to dollars and extending the fiscal adjustments and structural reforms initiated by his predecessors. In this way, he hoped to reduce the interest rate on local borrowings and the country risk premium[4] and promote economic activity, thereby increasing tax collections and building an operating fiscal surplus sufficient to restore confidence in the financial markets and prevent the repetition of the crises of 1989 and 1990.

In March 1991, Congress, at the instigation of the administration, enacted the Law of Convertibility, according to which the government was to convert 10,000 australs to one U.S. dollar (as of January 1, 1992, 10,000 australs were converted into one peso), inflationary indexation was prohibited, and the use of U.S. dollars was authorized as an accounting and transaction currency in the domestic economy. The law required foreign-currency-denominated financial assets of the central bank—such as gold, dollars, or other similarly solvent and convertible currencies, foreign securities, and national debt instruments denominated in foreign currency (valued at market prices)—to be at all times at least equal to the monetary base; in other words, the currency was to be backed up 100 percent by foreign-currency-denominated assets. Furthermore, the central bank assumed, by law, the obligation to sell currencies other than the national currency at a predetermined price, in amounts and at times freely chosen by economic agents.

At the same time, the government reached an agreement with the leading businesses setting voluntary price guidelines, launched a program of tax reform (aimed at eliminating distorting taxes, fighting tax evasion, and extending the applicability of the value-added tax) and government expenditure reductions, and achieved sustained progress toward structural reform (privatizations, deregulation, liberalization, and labor reform).

Results of the Economic Reform Programs

In general, the results of the convertibility program have been positive in terms of stabilization, levels of economic activity, fiscal adjustment, and the reordering of the economy. Annualized inflation, as measured by the consumer price index (CPI), fell from 431 percent in the first quarter of 1991, to 29 percent for the period from April to December 1991. The rate fell to 17.5 percent in 1992, 6.6 percent in 1993, and, on an annualized basis, to 3.9 percent during the first ten months of 1994. The fall in the wholesale price index, initially resulting from voluntary price agreements, and, later, from the pressure of international competition generated by the liberalization of trade, was even more dramatic. Inflation, as measured by the annualized wholesale price index, fell from 440 percent in the first quarter of 1991, to 2.8 percent for the rest of 1991, to 3.2 percent for 1992, to −0.8 percent for 1993, and, on an annualized basis, to 4.6 percent during the first ten months of 1994.

The high inflation regime that characterized Argentina in the 1970s and 1980s, the recurrent confiscations of the savings of the general public, and the hyperinflation crises of 1989–1990 caused the domestic capital and financial markets to atrophy. Increasingly, the majority of Argentines began to save a substantial part of their liquid assets in U.S. dollars. In mid-1989, it was estimated that Argentine investment abroad was approaching $45–50 billion, while the total value of the liquid assets of Argentines in the local financial sector (M3, plus deposits in dollars) and in the domestic capital market (market capitalization of shares, plus market value for liquid public and private debt instruments) was less than $14 billion; furthermore, a large portion of liquid savings was invested in dollar bills (an estimated $6 billion).[5] By the end of 1989, about 80 percent of Argentines' total liquid assets was invested in foreign financial instruments.

The economic reform program brought about a dramatic change in this trend. Remonetization of the economy has been gradual but steady. According to central bank data, the monetary base grew at an average monthly rate of 3.5 percent from April 1991 to December 1993, and had reached nearly 6 percent of GDP as of June 1994. The money supply, defined as M3, grew at an annual monthly rate of 4.1 percent for the same period and accounted for 12.5 percent of GDP as of October 1994. The government has provided incentives for the "dollarization" of the economy by letting all transactions (except tax and salary payments), as well as deposits and credits, be carried out in dollars or pesos indiscriminately. Deposits in dollars grew rapidly from $3.7 billion in April 1991, to approximately $22.3 billion as of October 30, 1994, about the same as deposits in pesos ($23.0 billion). Since a large number of the transactions between industries or for wholesale trade are made in dollars, it may be said that Argentina's economy now functions within the framework of a bi-monetary system. The domestic banking system's ability to extend loans (in dollars and pesos) increased from the equivalent of $4.8 billion in April 1991, to approximately $36.2 billion as of October 31, 1994, contributing to the strong increase in the demand for consumer durables and the recovery in levels of activity and investment that occurred during the period.

The capital market has benefited from a series of deregulatory measures and the reestablishment of stability. According to data provided by the Instituto Argentino del Mercada de Capitales, the equity market has grown rapidly. Capitalization of the market increased from $5 billion as of March 31, 1991, to approximately $19 billion as of March 31, 1993, and nearly $45 billion as of October 1994. The average volume of shares traded monthly on the Buenos Aires securities market went from $68 million in 1990, to approximately $1 billion in 1993 and fell to approximately $770 million during the first nine months of 1994.

In the past, the government debt was tax free, while the private sector debt was subject to discriminatory income, asset, and transfer taxes. The tax treatment for both government and private securities was equalized and a market for corporate bonds and commercial paper (*obligaciones negociables*) has developed; in 1991, there were placements for the equivalent of $550 million, in 1992 for approximately $1.6 billion, in 1993 for approximately $5.3 billion, and during the first nine months of 1994 for approximately 2.8 billion. In the equity market, the amount of new issues reached $851 million in 1991, $1.6 billion in 1992, approximately $5 billion in 1993, and $1.3 billion during the first nine months of 1994.

The size of the financial and capital markets has increased. Central bank data confirm that liquid assets (of banks and the capital market) in the domestic market, which accounted for approximately 20 percent of

GDP at the end of 1989, increased to almost 46 percent of GDP as of September 30, 1994. This figure continues to be very low compared to the domestic financial markets of industrialized countries (typically, bank credit and liquid assets of the capital market account for between 150 and 250 percent of GDP), but the progress that has been made is significant.

The domestic financial and capital markets are now completely integrated with the international markets since there are no restrictions of any kind on capital movements. But the domestic capital market suffers from the absence of domestic institutional investors (pension funds, mutual funds, and insurance companies). In this connection, it is enough to note that in the principal international capital markets, institutional investors control between 50 and 70 percent of the securities issued. The Mutual Investment Funds Law, recently implemented, and recent congressional approval (October 1993) of a system of private pension funds, which began operating in August 1994, will help to remedy this serious shortcoming in the medium term.

The recovery in the levels of industrial activity has been significant. According to central bank data, the seasonally adjusted industrial production index increased by 23 percent between March 1991 and August 1994. The industries with the greatest improvement were those involved in consumer durables, automobiles, and construction. For example, car production increased from 100,000 units in 1990, to 139,000 units in 1991, 262,000 in 1992, approximately 340,000 in 1993, and a forecasted 400,000 in 1994; purchases of refrigerators increased from 189,000 in 1989, to 421,000 in 1991, 715,000 in 1992, and 793,000 in 1993; and construction permits in the federal capital increased by more than 75 percent between January 1, 1991 and July 31, 1994.

The number of hours worked increased by 12.5 percent, and the economically active population increased by approximately 8.4 percent from May 1991 through May 1994. However, unemployment increased from an average of 6–7 percent in 1991 and 1992, to approximately 9.3 percent by the end of 1993, to 10.8 percent in mid-1994, due to dismissals resulting from privatizations, the reduction of public employees in the central administration, the contraction of certain inefficient private activities, and the restructuring and modernization of many private-sector enterprises (see table 4 in the appendix). In terms of economic growth, after two years of decline (1988–1989), and one of stagnation (1990), the economy recovered strongly, and it is estimated that real GDP grew at an annual rate of 8.9 percent in 1991, 8.7 percent in 1992, 6.0 percent in 1993, and an estimated 6 percent during 1994. Fixed investment recovered significantly, and it is estimated that it grew 25 percent in 1991, 31 percent in 1992, and 14 percent in 1993 and an estimated 13.5 percent in 1994. Gross investment, which had plummeted to an average level of 14.9 percent of GDP for the years 1989–1990, recovered to 16.3 percent in 1991, approximately 19 percent in 1992, and 21 percent in 1993.

The government has made a considerable effort to restore fiscal balance and recover access to voluntary credit. Progress toward a balanced budget has been very substantial. According to data provided by the Secretaria de Hacienda (the Treasury), the central bank's fiscal deficit has been substantially reduced, from an average of 3.5 percent of GDP for 1987, 1988, and 1989, to 1.0 percent in 1990, 0.6 percent in 1991, approximately 0.2 percent in 1992, and a slight surplus in 1993. The substantial improvement in fiscal revenues resulted in part from the recovery in levels of economic activity

TABLE 9. NATIONAL NONFINANCIAL PUBLIC SECTOR FISCAL PERFORMANCE[a]
(IN MILLIONS OF 1991 PESOS ADJUSTED FOR INFLATION: 1 PESO = 1 DOLLAR)

	1987	1988	1989	1990	1991	1992	1993
Current Revenue	28202	24406	21798	22882	29071	38768	44698
Total Expenditures	29880	26950	23319	20804	27772	35739	39722
Subtotal	−1678	−2544	−1521	2078	1299	3029	4977
Interest[b]	5185	4818	7631	5199	4744	3937	2914
Capital Revenue/Privatization	388	198	1104	569	2268	1892	668
Total (3 − 4 + 5)	−6475	−7164	−8048	−2552	−1177	985	2730

Sources: Ministerio de Economía, Secretaría de Hacienda, Informes y Gráficos sobre el comportamiento fiscal (1987–1994).
[a] Includes central government, decentralized agencies, social security and co-participation with provincial governments. Does not include quasi-fiscal central bank operations or provincial and municipal total revenue and expenditures. The data for 1987–March 1991 have been adjusted by inflation through April 1991.
[b] Interest on foreign debt is accrued. As for interest on domestic debt from 1985 to 1989, only the portion that corresponds to real interest (adjusted by inflation) is included.

referred to above and, in part, from tax reform that extended the applicability of the value-added tax and the income tax, as well as from improvements in tax administration and in enforcement against tax evasion, which has dropped considerably. Starting in 1991, the government began to reduce and/or eliminate inefficient taxes that distort production or have an anti-export bias (e.g., taxes on bank debits, taxes and fees on foreign trade, and stamp and asset taxes).

The government also made progress in its plan to reprogram foreign and domestic public debt. As of June 30, 1994, total foreign and domestic public debt amounted to about $70.2 billion, the equivalent of 27 percent of estimated GDP. Foreign public debt peaked at the end of 1989, when it reached the sum of $63.3 billion. The privatization program allowed for payments both in cash and in government debt, and resulted in the cancelation of almost $13.4 billion of debt between 1990 and 1993. At the end of 1993, foreign public debt had been reduced to $50.2 billion. Foreign public debt underwent long-term refinancing within the frameworks provided by the Brady Plan (commercial banks) and the Paris Club (export agencies). The Brady Plan for Argentina was implemented in April 1993, and consists of a 30-year refinancing, allowing for forgiveness of principal or interest, at the discretion of the creditor banks. Implementation of the plan formally reestablished relations between Argentina and creditor banks, facilitating the country's full re-entry into international credit markets and reducing the country's risk factor. Preliminary estimates for June 1994 indicate that the total level of public-sector external debt has not changed since the end of 1991, while private-sector external debt has increased rapidly by approximately $14 billion

Public domestic debt (in local and foreign currency) includes public securities originally placed with the investing public, as well as securities issued in recognition of accumulated unpaid liabilities owed to retired individuals, contractors, exporters, and beneficiaries of industrial promotion schemes. This debt is still being quantified, but the Secretaria de Hacienda has estimated that it equaled $20 billion at the end of June 1994 (not including foreign bonds, or BONEX, which are counted as part of the foreign debt). Beginning in 1993, the government initiated a program to gradually retire (through privatization sales) the long-term bonds (BOCONES) issued to pensioners.

In 1990, the federal government initiated a program to reduce the number of public employees of the central administration through compensated voluntary retirement. The number of public employees of the central administration was reduced to 435,000 in 1990, to approximately 346,000 at the end of 1992, and to approximately 319,000 at the end of 1993. The greatest reduction came about as a result of the transfer of 182,000 teachers to provincial jurisdictions. Of the other employee cuts, 34,000 were the result of normal retirement and 67,000 of voluntary retirement. It is estimated that the cost to the government of the voluntary retirement program for the years 1990–1992 was approximately $1.2 billion, or about $18,000 per retired employee. In the case of government-owned enterprises, whose total employment was approximately 347,000 in 1989, the privatization program in progress had reduced the number of employees to 66,700 by the end of 1993.

Provincial governments spend about 11 percent of GDP and finance their spending with resources transferred by the federal government (approximately 66 percent of the total) and with their own resources (approximately 33 percent of the total). Fiscal reform in the provincial sphere is still in the preliminary stages. Public employment in the provinces increased rapidly during the 1980s. Provincial public employees and employees for the municipality of Buenos Aires, for example, increased from 724,000 in 1980, to 1,014,000 in 1991. The number of provincial employees in 1993 reached 1,183,000, or approximately 10 percent of the economically active population. The provinces have made little progress in the deregulation of transportation, the liberal professions, and foreign trade. There is also a worrisome and growing deficit in the provincial social security systems, which was estimated at approximately $1.5 billion in 1993. With the support of the World Bank, the federal government intends to go forward with a restructuring of provincial finances to accompany efforts under way at the national level. The plan calls for a reduction of approximately 200,000 provincial employees. Similarly, the federal government wants to encourage the provinces to privatize the public enterprises under their authority (primarily electricity and natural gas distribution, waterworks, and provincial banking). The administration also wishes to give the provinces incentives to modernize their tax systems by eliminating stamp taxes, replacing taxes on gross income with a tax on final sales, and improving the administration of their tax systems. The implementation of these fiscal and administrative reforms at the provincial level will take time, especially in the poorer provinces where public employment functions as a kind of unemployment insurance.

With respect to the balance of payments, the stabilization program has produced some significant changes in underlying trends. The result for the balance of trade and real services was positive in the amount of $5.1 billion in 1989, $8 billion in 1990, and $2.8 billion in 1991.

But the balance of trade and real services turned around in 1992, with deficits of $3.9 billion in 1992, $4.9 billion in 1993, and a growing deficit of $5.8 billion is projected for 1994. This result was in response to a sharp increase in imports (from $8.3 billion in 1991, to $14.8 billion in 1992, $16.8 billion in 1993, and an estimated $21 billion during 1994), and a significant increase in spending on tourism (from $1.7 billion in 1991, to $2.2 billion in 1992, and $2.4 billion in 1993). The level of exports stabilized during 1990, 1991, and 1992. However, total exports increased during 1993 by about 9 percent and non-agricultural exports increased by about 13 percent. It is estimated that total exports during 1994 increased rapidly at a rate of approximately 18 percent.

The current account ran a deficit of $2.8 billion in 1991, $8.3 billion in 1992, $8.9 billion in 1993, and a projected $11.2 billion during 1994 (the equivalent of 3.9 percent of GDP). The capital account for the 1987–1993 period was financed by arrears in interest payments (1988–1991), programs of debt capitalization (1988–1989), net lending by international agencies (1987) and the Paris Club (1989, 1991), and, starting in the second half of 1990, by revenues from funds related to privatizations, the reopening of commercial bank credit and direct foreign investment, as well as short- and medium-term capital movements.

It is estimated that net inflow of private capital to Argentina in 1992 and 1993 (excluding that from international agencies and the Paris Club, government securities and loans, and arrears) reached a record high of $12 billion and $13.5 billion, respectively, a major increase from 1991, when the figure stood at $3.3 billion. The main engines of this sustained process of capital returns were privatizations, direct foreign investment, the reestablishment of foreign credit for foreign trade activities, medium-term bond issues and short-term portfolio in-

TABLE 10. EVOLUTION OF THE BALANCE OF PAYMENTS (1987–1992)

	1987	1988	1989	1990	1991	1992	1993
Current Account	−4235	−1572	−1305	1903	−2803	−8312	−8877
Goods							
Exports (FOB)	540	3810	5374	8275	3704	−2637	−3696
Imports (Cif)	6360	9134	9573	12354	11978	12235	13090
	5820	5324	4199	4079	8274	14872	16786
Real Services	−282	−255	−265	−321	−902[a]	−1054[a]	−1245[a]
Financial Services	−4485	−5127	−6422	−6122	−5634	−4589	−3872
Profits/Dividends	−558	−660	−664	−635	−805	−850	−986
Interest Received	218	211	265	280	379	439	676
Interest Accrued	−4145	−4678	6023	−5767	−5208	−4178	−3562
Unilateral Transfers	−8	0	8	71	29	−32	−64
Capital Account	3083	3648	−209	1444	5656	12090	13677
Direct Investment	−19[b]	1147	1028	305	465	442	628

Privatizations	0	0	0	1703	1974	4251	5611
Trade Financing	-541	-693	-5528	451	1758	3194	1032
Loans International Organization (Net)	1324	404	-71	304	204	-76	2028
Government Bonds and Loans	-96	-656	2618[c]	-1211	35[d]	-1128	-18594[e]
Paris Club (Net)	384	151	1402	372	697	324	412
Interest Arrears	39	2344	2927	1912	1788	884	-9276[e]
Private Bank Restructuring	1224	0	0	0	0	0	25589[e]
Other Operations (short term)	748	951	-5885	-2392	-857	4199	6247
Errors/ Omissions	-122	-115	-45	219	-125	-57	55
Fluctuations and Reserve Assets (+ = increment)	-1274	1961	-1559	3566	2728	3721	4855

Sources: Banco Central de la República Argentina, *Estimaciones Trimestrales del Balance de Pagos* (1987–1994).
[a] The increased deficit is mainly the result of tourism and foreign travel.
[b] Includes nationalization of Gasoducto Centro—Oeste.
[c] Includes placement of foreign bonds to cancel deposits in pesos in the financial system (the Bonex Plan).
[d] 1991 excludes placement of securities denominated in dollars to pay domestic debt.
[e] Results from the implementation of the Brady Plan.

vestments and capital movements, which increased dramatically in the second half of 1991 and in 1992 and stabilized during 1993. In the interim, the central bank accumulated reserves of $3.6 billion in 1990, $2.7 billion in 1991, $3.7 billion in 1992, $4.9 billion in 1993; during the first seven months of 1994 the stock of central bank reserves stabilized. The stock of reserves as of August 31, 1994, stood at $19 billion.

In general terms, the plan's success in reestablishing confidence can be measured by the fall in real interest rates. The rate for the country risk premium, measured as the difference between the domestic rate of return on the BONEX 1989 and the three-month London interbank offered rate, or LIBOR, fell from an average of approximately 20 percent in 1990, to 9.4 percent in 1991, 7.0 percent in 1992, and 4.2 percent in 1993, and increased to 5.6 percent during the first nine months of 1994.

STRUCTURAL REFORMS

The government of Argentina is committed to an ambitious program of structural reforms, the most important of which are privatizations, deregulation, labor reform, the restructuring of the social security system, trade liberalization, and regional integration. The remainder of this chapter will be devoted to a review of the progress made so far and the main issues pending in each of these areas.

Privatizations

In Argentina, the government's role as a producer of goods and services has been very significant in recent decades. Over the last fifteen years, government-owned enterprises accounted for 7 percent of GDP, 3 to 4 percent of total employment, and 21 percent of total gross investment, and their total spending in current and capital accounts has represented approximately 15 to 18 percent of GDP.[6] This extensive government intervention in business activities was the result of a vision shared by the main political forces in the country. This vision, which we could call "productivist and statist," favored government support of development through subsidies, the control of natural resources, and a government monopoly with respect to public services and key industrial activities.[7] The necessity for state control of public services and industries was based on the assumption that such services and industries had a strategic value in the process of development and should therefore not be provided by the private sector, which in any case had neither the financial resources nor the long-term horizon necessary to carry out the required investments.

Although this strategy worked for a while (the government invested the necessary resources so that public services kept pace with increases in the level of economic activity), serious inefficiencies gradually accumulated in the allocation of resources. These inefficiencies originated mainly in the fixing of rates for public services in order to stabilize or distribute income and the enormous volatility of these rates over time. These price distortions caused overinvestment in some sectors and underinvestment in others, and often encouraged the increase of consumption through the provision of goods and services at prices below cost. Furthermore, government-owned enterprises exhibited low levels of efficiency and productivity in their business operations, no doubt a result of the high level of protection these enterprises enjoyed from local and foreign competition. The postal monopoly of ENCOTEL; the "flag carrier" status of Aerolineas Argentinas, with its legal control of 60 percent of the country's domestic routes; and prohibitions against the entry of outside competitors in the natural gas, electricity, and water sectors are cases in point. The management processes at government-owned enterprises were "colonized" over time, taken over by suppliers, users, unions, and officials who maximized the benefits to themselves at the cost of the enterprises' efficiency and productivity.

In general, the productivity of capital in Argentina's public sector has been extremely low.[8] For example, the cost per phone line installed by ENTEL during the 1970–1991 period was approximately $4,600 (in 1991 prices), as compared to international costs on the order of $1,500–2,000. For the same period, the unit cost (per kilowatt) of investment in the electricity sector was approximately $6,600, compared to international costs ranging from $1,500 to $2,700, and energy losses due to user fraud reached a level of 30 percent, when they should not, by international standards, have exceeded 10 percent. In a detailed study of four sectors (electricity, railroads, waterworks, and telephones), FIEL found an excess of expenditures above normal levels on the order of 45 percent for the 1970–1991 period.

To finance their investments and part of their current expenses, government-owned enterprises have relied heavily on contributions from the Treasury and domestic and foreign indebtedness, and they have contributed significantly to the severe fiscal crisis that has devastated the Argentine government in recent decades. In 1989, the Directorate of Public Enterprises estimated that the accumulated demand for financing for the 1965–1987 period on the part of the biggest government-owned enterprises was as high as $52 billion, equivalent to approximately 90 percent of the stock of foreign debt for 1988. It is estimated that the average need for financing of government-owned enterprises during the period in question added to the government's fiscal deficit by more than 3 percent of GDP per year.

In the mid-1980s, the public began to see that government-owned enterprises were not fulfilling their role. Their contribution to growth was declining, productivity from investments was low, corruption was widespread, and the quality of services was in serious decay. People also became aware that public enterprises were a no-man's-land, where suppliers, unions, users, and officials held sway, generally at the expense of the rest of society.

The first attempts to privatize public firms (ENTEL and Aerolineas Argentinas) occurred during the last two years of the Radical government (1988–1989). The failure of these attempts, in conjunction with the sharp decline in the quality of services, helped make a very broad sector of the public aware of the problems associated with government-owned enterprises generally.

The privatization program now underway is a highly ambitious one. It aims to transfer to the private sector practically all public services, as well as government-owned companies in the more competitive environments (trade, industry, transport, services). Its key objectives are:

- to reduce the fiscal deficit arising from the government-owned enterprise sector;
- to transfer government economic activities into private hands, with the aim of improving the management of the resources involved, raising the quality of services, and curbing the pressures that such corporatist groups as contractors, unions, large users, and management bring to bear (thus reducing fraud and the other dishonest behavior that characterizes such activities);

- to make future investment more efficient by rehabilitating public services and modernizing industrial activities;
- to use privatization as a means of payment for reducing the domestic and foreign public debt and for reestablishing the government's fiscal solvency;
- to free up limited financial and managerial capacity in the public sector for more important uses that offer a higher rate of economic and social return, such as health care, education, public safety, and justice.

According to the undersecretary for privatizations, as of December 31, 1993, the government had sold 64 firms or business units; among the largest were the oil company YPF, ENTEL, Aerolineas Argentinas, various electric companies (such as SEGBA and part of Agua y Energía), Gas del Estado, steel companies (such as SOMISA and ZAPLA), petrochemical and defense industries (such as POLISUR, INDUCLOR, Monomoros Vinilicos, Petroquímica Río Tercero, and TANDANOR), as well as race tracks and hotels (Llao Llao). There had also been 790 sales of real estate. The government has granted concessions to 19 firms, principally in the following areas: waterworks (Obras Sanitarias de la Nación), railroads (almost 25,000 kilometers), the Buenos Aires subway, tolls on 34 national highways (10,000 kilometers), television and radio stations, and wholesale markets, such as the Mercado de Liniers. Concessions were also granted for 86 secondary oil zones, and partnership contracts were signed by YPF and private companies for the development of 9 central zones. YPF sold several refineries, pipelines, and part of its fleet of ships. In the third quarter of 1993, the government sold 70 percent of the shares of YPF in a public equity issue that was placed simultaneously in Argentina

and the international capital markets, raising approximately $3 billion and canceling $1.3 billion of public
debt. In addition, during the second semester of 1993 the
government privatized several power-generation facilities (Chocon, Cerros Colorados, Piedra del Aguila, and
Alicura) raising approximately $345 million in cash and
canceling $580 million of public debt. The administra-
tion of harbors was transferred to the provincial governments, and a new port law was passed to facilitate the
creation of private ports. The inefficient and high-cost
port of Buenos Aires is being divided into 6 independent
private terminals. The government also assigned to the
private sector the tasks of setting up and running the
domestic satellite telecommunications system and
dredging and placing navigational markers in the Parana
River and the Rio de la Plata.

The government expects to conclude the initial
phase of the privatization program during 1995. The
main enterprises to be privatized during this period include the government shipbuilding firm (ELMA), the
postal service, several power stations of Agua y Energía
Eléctrica and Hidronor, Petroquímica Mosconi, Petroquímica Bahía Blanca, Indupa, the General Belgrano
Railway (10,800 km), the major airports, and a number
of military factories. The government has also assigned
additional concessions to the private sector for highway
networks giving access to the big cities, as well as for
various national routes. In the financial sector, during
the first half of 1994, the National Bank of Savings and
Insurance was transferred to the private sector, and an
effort is underway to transfer the mint during 1995.
Approximately 3,200 real estate properties are for sale,
as are various grain elevators and silos located in exporting ports. The government plans to privatize the National Atomic Energy Commission power stations in 1995.

TABLE 11. THE PRIVATIZATION PROGRAM: 1990–1993
TRANSACTIONS COMPLETED

	1990	1991	1992	1993	Total
Enterprises Sold	6	2	25	31	64
Services Licensed	3	7	9	—	19
Oil Concessions	37	22	27	—	86
Oil Contracts	5	4	—	—	9
Market Sale of Shares	—	1	1	3	2
Revenues Received (US$ million)					
Income in Cash	1288	2348	1970	4130	9736
Debt Instruments (face value)	4165	2440	3039	2205	11849
Liabilities Transferred	—	—	1576	—	1576

Sources: Ministry of Economy, Under Secretary of Privatization (April 1994).

Beginning in 1995, the government intends to sell gradually in the capital markets all or part of the shares it had kept for itself in certain key privatizations—in YPF and in the new privatized natural gas and electric transportation and distribution companies. The value of the blocks of shares for sale in the public market that remain in the hands of the government and that could be placed in the securities markets is difficult to estimate at present, since it will depend on the evolution of these businesses and, particularly, on the quality of management of their new owners. However, I estimate that during the next two years the privatization program (including the sale of the public equity mentioned above) could generate revenues of approximately $3 billion in cash and $3 billion in public-debt cancellation.

With respect to the purchasers' origins, the undersecretary for privatizations has estimated that as of June 30, 1993, approximately 57 percent were investors from abroad. Among these, 15 percent were from the United States and Canada, 13.5 percent were from Spain, 8.3 percent were from Italy, 6.4 percent were from France, 5.6 percent were from Chile, and the remaining 8.2 percent were from other developed countries. If these proportions remain constant during the 1994 privatizations, and estimates of direct foreign investment for 1994 of $1 billion prove correct, the stock of foreign investment in the country, which was estimated to be approximately $10 billion in mid-1989,[9] will have more than doubled in the space of five years.

Purchasers have usually been consortia of firms formed by domestic groups with the business acumen to appreciate the worth of these businesses and the management and financial capabilities to participate in them, as well as foreign firms that contributed technology, know-how, and capital, foreign banks, local public works contractors who capitalized unpaid public foreign and domestic debt, and a large group of local and foreign investors. In certain areas, such as highway concessions, television and radio stations, leisure activities, and the sale of real estate, most investments were made by domestic firms and investors.

According to data provided by the undersecretary for privatizations, the degree of economic concentration resulting from these privatizations does not appear to be excessive. Although it is true that certain local groups have acquired a significant portion of shares sold—the largest being Perez Companc/Banco Rio, which bought 13.9 percent of the assets sold; Techint, which bought 7 percent; Astra, 5.2 percent; Sideco, 2.6 percent; and Comercial del Plata, 2 percent—their participation is generally distributed among several investments and made in association with other domestic and foreign groups.

The introduction of new foreign investors to the domestic economy, including first-rate international firms, and the creation of numerous new private firms in sectors of activity that were previously entirely closed to competition, portend an increase of competitive pressures in the economy. It is estimated that more than 80 new businesses have been created in the petroleum sector alone. In the power generation and distribution sector, the 3 original government companies have been broken up into 25 new private companies. In the natural gas sector, the Gas del Estado monopoly has been broken up into 15 independent pipeline and distribution companies. If we note that private management of these assets has increased the number and variety of suppliers, we can begin to glimpse the real impact of privatization on competition and economic concentration.

The fiscal effects of the program of privatization have also been positive. The government received large cash revenues ($9.7 billion, as of June 30, 1994), and did away with a series of firms and activities that in general were operating with big losses and faced acute future financing needs to implement their investment programs. The privatization program has also made it possible to retire large amounts of domestic and foreign public debt ($13.4 billion, as of June 30, 1994), and helped to reestablish the government's solvency and reduce long-term interest rates and the country risk premium. It is estimated that by the end of 1995, assuming that the government completes its plans, the privatization program will have generated at least $13 billion in cash and allowed the retirement of approximately $16 billion in public debt. Although domestic taxation on certain public rates (with respect to ENTEL and the oil sector) has been reduced, which resulted in an immediate decline in government revenue, it is estimated that the payment of fees by concession holders, taxes on profits, and other corporate taxes will generate a significantly higher flow of revenue in the future.

The Argentine privatization program is certainly the most ambitious in Latin America. However, it needs to be extended to the provincial governments, which are still well behind in their efforts to privatize a fairly large number of provincial government-owned banks and companies (primarily electrical, water, and gas companies). When it is completed, Argentina will rank with those countries with the least government intervention in productive activities. In this it will more closely resemble the United States than western Europe, where government economic activity still plays an important role.

This dramatic reduction of government economic activity presents Argentine society with the extraordinary opportunity to acquire efficiency and competitiveness. Through the creation of sophisticated, cost-conscious demand, privatization will provide a decisive impetus to the modernization of various industrial sectors and services supplying the newly privatized companies. The breakup of oligopolistic arrangements and the reintroduction of competition in terms of price and quality will produce profound changes in business behavior and in the levels and quality of investment.

There are already indications that Argentina will develop significant export activities in private-sector natural gas and oil. (A privately sponsored oil pipeline to Chile began operations during the first quarter of 1994, and negotiations on several natural gas export projects with Chile and Brazil are at advanced stages.) This export activity will certainly extend to industrial sectors and services supplying the newly privatized companies, which, over time, will undoubtedly be in the technological vanguard of their respective sectors in Latin America. It is estimated that in the future public investment in infrastructure will fall to less than 25 percent of total investment in activities previously controlled by the government.[10] The public sector maintains a large interest in investment in the electricity sector (in the completion of the hydroelectric Yacireta power station and the nuclear facility, Atucha II), in the construction and maintenance of national roads with low traffic density, and in the extension of water and sewage services to low-income and low-population-density areas.

But privatization also presents the country, and the government in particular, with a significant organizational challenge. A privatized economy is undoubtedly an economy in which business efficiency and the productivity of future investments will be high. But it is also an economy exposed to heavy losses of efficiency in the allocation of resources, at the level of the economy as a whole, if the structure of markets in which the newly privatized firms operate is either monopolistic or strongly oligopolistic or if the regulatory frameworks and/or their functioning are insufficient to protect the interests of consumers and business users in the long term.

During the next few years, Argentina will have to face the difficulties of regulating private monopolies and ensuring a fair representation of consumers' interests. The need to increase competition and restructure tariff schedules is particularly obvious in the cases of Aerolíneas Argentinas and the new private telephone companies. If the regulatory mechanisms that protect users are inadequate, or if the authorities entrusted with applying such mechanisms do not fulfill their responsibilities, there is a risk that future increases of produc-

tive efficiency and the benefits that result from the reduction of capital costs that should be transferred to the
users will be transfered instead to the production factors
that are part of a monopolistic delivery system of public
services (shareholders, workers, executives, and suppliers). Users could face a structure of excessively high
rates or prices, which would distort relative domestic
prices, penalize other productive sectors, and reduce
real wages in the rest of the economy, thus adversely
affecting resource allocation and growth potential for
the economy over the long term. Despite some initial
delays, "regulatory commissions" for the electricity, natural gas, telephone, railway, and water and sewage sectors are already in operation. It is still too early to
appraise their effectiveness.

Deregulation

Through the control of key macroeconomic variables—
prices, wages, interest rates, and payments and receipts
in foreign currencies—and control and regulation of a
broad range of markets, products, and production factors, Argentina's government tried to guarantee prices
and revenues and determine the working of markets and
relationships between economic agents, subsidizing or
penalizing private investments and activities. But it is
known that regulations, when they are unnecessary or
excessive, can adversely affect the performance of the
private sector and cause serious losses of efficiency and
disrupt the well-being of society as a whole. This has
certainly been the case in Argentina, where the myriad
government regulations negatively distorted resource
allocation (in terms of cost or loss of economic efficiency), diminished competition (at a cost of reduced
innovation), increased private-sector operating costs
(delivery costs), and increased government expendi-

tures (administrative costs). Government regulation contributed significantly to the deterioration of the institutional framework, encouraging the transfer of resources from the formal to the underground economy, increasing uncertainty, and spreading corruption.

Market weaknesses, or rather, the inability of market mechanisms to provide certain goods efficiently due to externalities, monopolies, and the existence of "public goods," may under certain circumstances require government regulatory action. Nevertheless, analysis of Argentina's regulatory universe indicates that many of the regulations introduced in recent decades arose from the desire to compensate for fundamental macroeconomic imbalances—fiscal, monetary, and/or balance of payment—through administrative means. Other regulations grew out of the impulse to protect firms in decline, restrain competition, and generate transfers of revenues to favored activities. This generalized application of regulation coincided with the government's growing inability to exercise its genuine functions of regulation and control in the areas of health, safety, environmental protection, and promotion of competition.

The economic reform in progress has eliminated almost all macroeconomic price controls and regulations. Between July 1989 and January 1991, wage controls were abolished, price controls were liberalized, and exchange controls (on movements in both the current account and in the capital account) were eliminated entirely. A second phase of deregulation began in 1991. The monopoly rights of existing wholesale distribution markets for internal trade in goods and services were eliminated, and the opening of new wholesale markets was authorized. Additionally, a number of regulations restricting retail trade were eliminated, including restrictions on starting new businesses and on business hours.

In the area of retail and wholesale trade, competition has intensified and new forms of marketing are rapidly spreading in the big urban centers. An attempt was made to enhance competition in the liberal professions by liberalizing the procedures of market entry and/or certification and fee-setting. To increase competition in the market for pharmaceutical products approval procedures were simplified for new products and import products that had already been approved in advanced industrial countries with higher health-control standards than Argentina. Moreover, pharmacies may now be freely opened.

Ten regulatory agencies in the sector of primary activities were dissolved. The National Meat Board, the Meat Producers Corporation, and the Liniers Cattle Market were dissolved or privatized. The National Forest Institute, the Regulatory Commission and the Central Market for Yerba Mate, the National Sugar Board, and the Central Fish Market were also dissolved. As these and other such agencies were eliminated, their respective regulatory mechanisms, including the purchase or selling of monopolies and restrictions on the entry of new competitors, quotas, and price supports were eliminated, as were twelve taxes or rates charged on regulated activities.

In the insurance market, the government monopoly on reinsurance was suppressed, regulations restricting competition in both products and premium rates were revised, and the modernization of the Insurance Administration was initiated so that it might be able to supervise more effectively the solvency and operating performance of insurance companies.

With respect to oil, in the past the government fixed prices, set margins for refineries and service stations, controlled foreign-trade operations, monopolized the sale and purchase of crude, and required authorization for the establishment of service stations. The reform program in the oil sector has deregulated prices, margins, and foreign- and domestic-trade operations, and has eliminated production quotas and production-sharing agreements. The sale by YPF of numerous oil fields and the renegotiation of existing service contracts transferred the management of a large portion of Argentina's oil industry to the private sector. Crude oil production reached a historic high in 1993, with total production increasing by approximately 22 percent over 1991 levels.

With respect to investment, sectoral promotion schemes for the steel, shipbuilding, and aeronautics industries have been eliminated. Foreign investment in both the mining and transportation sectors has been completely liberalized. Rules requiring prior government authorization for foreign investment have also been done away with, and domestic and foreign investment have been put on an equal footing with regard to tax treatment.

In the capital market, commissions were deregulated to increase competition among brokers, taxes on transactions were eliminated, and requirements for the issuance of new financial assets were simplified. Legislation to permit and facilitate the issuance of new financial products, such as corporate bonds, commercial paper, futures, collateralized obligations, and swaps was passed, as was a law making mutual investment funds operations more flexible.

Competition was fostered in the passenger transportation sector by permitting bus firms already providing services in one area to offer services without prior authorization in transit corridors where other firms are already operating. Deregulation at the federal level of ground freight transport promoted competition by eliminating the need for special trucking licenses and the requirement that freight had to be carried on trucks from the area where the freight originated.

With respect to ports and river and maritime navigation, all labor contracts were suspended, various regulatory agencies were dissolved, and navigation services such as harbor pilotage, river pilotage, and towing were deregulated. Management and labor monopolies on land services were done away with, and entrepreneurs are now permitted to decide on the makeup of crews, insurance, and other operational aspects of the business. Competition was also encouraged by removing the obligation to use vessels flying the national flag in traffic between national ports.

The program of deregulation has reduced costs and fiscal pressure on productive activities. In sectors where cost reduction has been significant, pressure by users has been decisive. For example, costs have fallen considerably in such sectors as shipping, ports, and ground-freight transport because shipowners, trucking companies, and large users have exerted pressure. In automotive passenger transport, the number of suppliers increased and, as a result, prices fell and the quality and variety of services improved. Ground-freight transport costs to Brazil fell by almost 30 percent. According to government estimates, the real rate of exchange has improved between 2 percent and 4 percent, depending on the sector.[11] This improvement will strengthen the profitability of the export sector.

Over the medium term, the deregulation that has already occurred will deeply affect costs, prices, and rates, increase sectoral competition, accelerate technological innovation, and increase the variety of services and products supplied to different markets. But there is still a long list of items on the regulatory agenda that need to be changed. The modification of the rules of the game did not result in automatic or immediate changes in all markets—especially not in those markets in which institutional inertia or monopolistic practices resist change, where, for example, the staff of governmental agencies and users continue to comply with abolished regulations. It has also been very difficult to deregulate prices for professional services because of the continued opposition by professional schools and associations. Lawyers, accountants, auctioneers, architects, and notaries have taken refuge in provincial and municipal regulations to preserve their privileges, such as the centralized collection of fees, fixed rates, and restrictions on entry into their professions. A range of provincial and municipal regulations mainly affecting freight and passenger transport, food and medicine, and regional products are still in effect. Loading-ramp and warehouse services at the principal airports continue to operate within a monopolistic framework, increasing prices and undermining the export potential of various sectors. Domestic airline fares are very high by international standards. Finally, despite the government's deregulatory efforts, bureaucratic and administrative procedures have not been simplified, heavily penalizing small and medium-sized businesses and industries.

Labor and Social Security Reform

The interventionist state model of a closed economy with a high degree of government meddling in the processes of capital accumulation, resource allocation, and income distribution has as a corollary organizational patterns in labor relations and the administration of social assistance programs that are dysfunctional and/or prejudicial to the functioning of an open capitalist economy with the potential for sustained growth.

In postwar Argentina, labor regulation became the vehicle for crystallizing union power and balancing the economic power enjoyed by the business sector in the absence of strong domestic and foreign competition. In this way, the corporatist state granted organized labor a political channel through which to participate in the struggle for the distribution of income.

Argentina's labor market was extensively regulated following the military coup of 1943 and during the first Perón administration (1945–1955) as a means of gaining the confidence of the labor unions and strengthening their relationship with the government. During the following three decades, this regulatory regime was maintained, even though it was recognized as a potential brake on economic growth and a source of substantial political and economic power for labor-union leaders.

The original aim of these regulations was to increase pay and improve working conditions for wage earners, but over the long term they led to rigidities in Argentina's postwar labor system. Only one union is recognized for each branch of activity. Union membership is not compulsory by law, but in practice it is obligatory through the rules of collective-bargaining agreements, which have the force of law. Centralized collective bargaining for entire branches of economic activity inhibits firms from negotiating on the basis of the specific conditions of the markets in which they operate and from adapting to the changing conditions of competition and to technological change. Labor disputes resulting from collective bargaining are regulated by binding arbitration, which confers discretionary legal powers on the government. Labor contracts are usually of indefinite duration, and contracts of limited duration are severely restricted—temporary employment is illegal except in authorized cases—which has adversely affected the demand for labor, particularly among young people, women, and the unemployed. Job-security guarantees hinder the mobility of resources from less productive to more productive sectors, as do the costs of dismissal—the usual indemnification is two months' salary for each year worked—and the lack of unemployment insurance and retraining programs, which might facilitate the transfer of labor to more productive sectors. Regulations that limit the distribution of the hours of the work week and job assignments within firms hamper effective human-resource management.

The adverse effects on economic growth of a system of labor regulation like Argentina's are hard to quantify, since the regulations impinge upon an infinite number of individual decisions. Nevertheless, it is clear that such a system does not foster innovation and technological change or create conditions in which the intensification of foreign and domestic competition results in greater efficiency and new investment. Encouraging training and the mobility of human resources, decentralizing wage negotiations, and promoting broad cooperation between wage earners and management to increase productivity are indispensable for sustained increases of real wages for workers and sustained economic growth over the long term. With such goals in mind, the government has initiated negotiations with the labor unions and the employer federations to introduce in Congress, during 1994–1995, a labor deregulation law that would correct some of the perverse effects of the existing labor regulation system. However, since the labor unions provide important political support for the government, and presidential elections are scheduled for mid-1995, it is highly unlikely that a major breakthrough regarding labor deregulation will occur before the end of 1995.

TABLE 12. EMPLOYER'S AND EMPLOYEE'S CONTRIBUTION TO THE SOCIAL SECURITY SYSTEM

WHERE CONTRIBUTIONS GO	EMPLOYER %	EMPLOYEE %	TOTAL %	CONTRIBUTIONS % NET SALARIES
Social Insurance	16.0	10.0	26.0	31.0
Family Aid	7.5	0.0	7.5	8.9
Unemployment Insurance	1.5	0.0	1.5	1.8
Social Assistance	9.0	5.0	14.0	16.7
Union Contributions	—	1.0	1.0	1.2
TOTAL	34.0	16.0	50.0	59.5

Source: Daniel Artana and Ricardo Lopez Murphy, "Un Sistema Tributario para el Crecimiento," in Felipe A.M. de la Balze, *Reforma y Convergencia* (Buenos Aires: CARI/Manantial, 1993), p. 207.

Another cause for concern is the high nonwage labor costs that characterize Argentina's labor markets. The gap between remuneration actually received by workers and total labor employment expenses assumed by employers is very great, and management costs and payments made by individuals to social security and other social assistance programs are very high. In general, these payments are effectively labor taxes, since the relationship between payments and benefits received by the worker is tenuous. Social charges, which in Argentina account for approximately 50 percent of gross wages, are high when compared to Australia, Spain, Holland, Switzerland, and the United States, where they account for approximately 30 percent of gross wages. These taxes negatively affect resource allocation, reduce the demand for labor, discriminate against exports (GATT rules do not permit government reimbursements to exporters for such taxes), and encourage the growth of the informal economy (off-the-books employment). The Ministry of Labor estimates that out of a total of approximately 12 million workers, only 7.5 million are formally registered. The existence of such a large group of nonregistered workers distorts the functioning of labor markets and increases costs for businesses that operate in the formal economy. During 1993 and 1994, the government reduced employers' social contributions in certain sectors (industry, agriculture, and mining) in provinces that have agreed to reform their fiscal and administration policies. The government has indicated that it plans, if budgetary constraints permit, to extend such benefits gradually to all employers during 1995.

A third element that raises the cost of labor and undermines the competitiveness of Argentina's economy is the high degree of combativeness and litigiousness that characterizes labor relations. While this has resulted in limited benefits for workers, it has generated tensions and uncertainties that reduce the demand for labor and incorporate an additional cost that is difficult to assess. One study of a large number of firms from 1988 to 1990 estimated that payments for work accidents (including insurance premiums) represented almost 2 percent of gross payroll.[12] The Law of Accidents at Work was amended to put some limits on employers' liability and on damages awarded, as well as on fees for lawyers and legal experts. However, the changes introduced are insufficient (as a result of opposition by unions and lawyers' associations), and the government is attempting to obtain congressional approval for a more substantive reform program.

So far, the government has taken a number of steps to deregulate the labor market. In 1990, a new employment law was passed, but, unfortunately, it did not correct the serious defects of the system. Union prerogatives were maintained, wage negotiations were not decentralized, and, although certain flexible mechanisms for contracting temporary work were created, they remained within the framework of industry-wide collective bargaining rather than on the level of the individual firm. According to the Ministry of Labor, only 14,000 people joined the labor force in 1992 as a result of the temporary work contracts put forward by the new law. The right of public-service employees in hospitals, transportation, utilities, and the judicial system to strike was regulated to guarantee the provision of a minimal level of service. All collective bargaining agreements for government enterprises in the process of privatization were repudiated and are being renegotiated by their new managements. In settled cases, internal administrative restrictions with no rational basis that penalized productivity and boosted wage costs have been substantially reduced. A modest number of programs have been started to upgrade and retrain the work force and to facilitate the relocation of workers who have lost their jobs. These programs are financed by the capitalization and deferment of severance benefits for workers who voluntarily join the program. Salary increases in the framework of collective bargaining agreements were pegged to increases in productivity, and a cap was placed on the indexing adjustments that had characterized such agreements in the past, stimulating inflation.

These steps have had the greatest impact on privatized public enterprises, especially with respect to curbs on litigation concerning accidents at work and the restrictions on nonproductivity-related wage increases. If Argentina truly wishes to reduce production costs, better allocate available resources, and establish an institutional framework that allows it to compete with the rest of the world, it will have to democratize the union structure, allowing more than one union per activity or per region; amend the Employment Law to make contracting more flexible, thus promoting the employment of young people and women; decentralize labor negotiations to the individual firm level and eliminate the government's role in binding arbitration in conflicts between labor and management; eliminate severance benefits for employees who have worked for short periods and for people under twenty years of age; significantly reduce taxes on labor to no more than 30 percent of gross wages, and reform in depth the Law of Accidents at Work.

The social security system accounts for the greatest government expenditure. Pension, retirement, and health benefits (national and provincial) reached 11.3 percent of GDP in 1993, and amounted to almost 38 percent of consolidated public-sector expenditures for that year. Social security has been based on a "distribution system," in which pensions are paid by the contributions of active workers, supplemented, if necessary, by the government. Early signs of the social security system's exhaustion became apparent in the 1970s. During the next decade, the imbalances became worse and the system went into a severe crisis. A growing gap between revenues and expenditures (including amounts owed but not paid). due to patterns of aging and increasing evasion of payments, generated an average fiscal deficit from 1989 to 1992 roughly equal to 2 percent of GDP.[13] The tenuous link between contributions made today and future retirement benefits, along with the high tax burden on labor, have combined to produce a low ratio of contributors to beneficiaries, which was estimated at 1.6:1 in 1991. The evasion rate may be as high as 50 percent, considering that close to 4.5 million workers do not contribute to the system, and many who do contribute do so for only a portion of their real earnings.[14]

Administrative costs of the social security system have also been very high, ranging from 2.5 to 3.5 percent of the system's total revenue. The lack of managerial skill has given rise to fraud, resulting in payment of benefits to dead people, to beneficiaries older than 130 years of age, and to an excessive number of retired individuals who declare themselves to be disabled (17 percent of the total).

The most serious problem of the current system is that there is no clear relationship between what employees pay into the system and their future retirement and disability insurance benefits. This lack of connection discourages individual and family savings, encourages evasion, and discourages a sense of personal responsibility. The evolution of Argentina into a society in which individuals and families undertake to plan for the needs of old age, disability, and premature death will undoubtedly be a more evolved society, one in which individuals will act more responsibly, not only in the context of their jobs and family life, but also as citizens.

The government's proposal for the reform of the social security system was approved by the National Congress in September 1993 and took effect in August 1994. In the future, social security will be based on a distribution system administered by the government, combined with a system of "capitalization" administered by the private sector. The distribution system will grant roughly similar retirement benefits for each beneficiary, somewhere on the order of 30 to 40 percent of the average wage—a reduced but universal pension for all who have contributed for a minimum of 30 years—thus incorporating an element of income redistribution and social solidarity. The system of capitalization will be organized through private pension funds, and contributors are able to choose the pension fund they prefer and change funds when they like. The minimum retirement age has been raised to 65 years, and individual contributions will represent 11 percent of the contributor's wages. During the period of transition from the old system to the new, payments to beneficiaries of the old system will be financed by the government. The total monthly contributions to the system will likely total approximately $300 million, of which approximately $155 million are being capitalized in the new pension funds. As of September 30, 1994, approximately 2.0 million employees had joined the new private pension fund system. The private pension funds expect a much larger number of employees to gradually join the new system during the next two years, as the new procedures become better known by the public at large. The main economic and social benefits of the new system will be seen in increased national savings, greater individual responsibility for retirement planning, and greater institutional investment in the local capital market.

A positive effect on overall savings rates for the economy can reasonably be expected, although it is very hard to predict the magnitude of such an effect. Undoubtedly, the accumulation of large amounts of money under the administration of the new pension funds will increase available resources in the domestic capital market—according to the Ministry of Economy estimates, resources administered by the funds could reach $25 billion by the year 2000—although this in itself would not prove that economic agents were increasing their rates of real savings. Nevertheless, other countries' success in these matters, as well as the absence, during the past decades of high inflation, of reliable institutional mechanisms to encourage and channel the savings of the general public in Argentina, lead me to believe that the effect on savings rates of such an institutional reform will probably be very considerable indeed.

Similarly, the large fiscal deficits resulting from the need to finance social security benefits with public resources will gradually diminish. For a relatively prolonged period of time the government will have to finance the provision of services linked to the "old" system, as well as fund the new distribution system and service payments on the bonds issued to retired individuals as payment for unpaid amounts. This so-called pension assistance debt is an estimated $10 billion as of mid-1994. But, as has been the case in Chile for some years, a substantial part of the capitalized resources in the new system will be invested in long-term government securities, which will help to finance the system's transitional deficit.

The creation of a new private pension system cannot solve the accumulated financial and fiscal problems of the previous system, though it can certainly help to reduce government expenditures by combating the extremely high rate of evasion of social security contributions in recent decades. The government pension deficit will also diminish as a consequence of the new retirement age of 65 years.

The reform of social security will generate abundant resources in the long term that could be allocated to finance productive investments both in the private and public sectors. The new system is generating a network of institutional investors with the technical and professional ability to analyze projects and commit to the financing of long-term investments. No doubt the new system of private pension funds will help to broaden, modernize, and render more professional the domestic capital market, which will then be able to attract investors from abroad and make the process of transferring savings to investment more efficient. This, in time, will stimulate the country's growth rate.

With respect to health care benefits, it will be necessary to deregulate the system of "social health benefits" (*obras sociales*). These benefits, mostly controlled by the unions, provide medical services and other forms of social assistance to approximately 17 million members. The system's most serious weakness, which should be remedied as soon as possible, is the captive status of members. Proposed deregulation would make it possible for members to choose freely from among social/health assistance plans, which, in turn, should give rise to genuine competition in the delivery of services and provide incentives to private providers and health insurance companies and/or unions to form new entities. The labor unions have strongly opposed the deregulation of the social/health benefits system, but the government has indicated its intention to send a reform package to Congress during 1995.

Regional Integration and the Liberalization of Trade

A movement toward closer economic cooperation between Argentina and Brazil has gained momentum in recent years. In June 1986, Argentina and Brazil launched the Program of Economic Cooperation and Integration, aimed at increasing bilateral trade flows and establishing closer economic ties between the two largest South American economies. Argentina and Brazil signed a bilateral treaty in 1988 creating a common market (MERCOSUR), and in March 1991, Paraguay and Uruguay joined the effort to establish the common market by the end of 1994. Bilateral trade between Argentina and Brazil has grown from $1.4 billion in 1986, to $2.1 billion in 1990, to $6.4 billion in 1993. Bilateral trade as a percentage of the total foreign trade of Brazil and Argentina has grown from 2.9 percent in 1986, to 3.2 percent in 1990, to 7.2 percent in 1993. Argentina's exports to Brazil have diversified toward manufactures, from 22 percent of total sales in 1985, to 57 percent in 1993. Agreed-upon automatic across-the-board tariff cuts have been introduced.

A lack of macroeconomic policy coordination, however, has produced large fluctuations in bilateral real exchange rates and wide shifts in competitiveness, and has weakened the effects of trade liberalization on the expansion of trade and investment in the enlarged market. Argentina imposed an additional tariff (the statistical fee) in 1992 to reduce Brazilian imports,[15] and Brazil has been slow to remove its numerous nontariff barriers to Argentine exports. Furthermore, the macroeconomic instability and policy volatility exhibited by both countries until 1991, and mostly by Brazil since then, has created an unfriendly economic climate for economic integration.

If a fully operational common market is unlikely to emerge in 1994, the establishment of a free trade area and an imperfect customs union seem to be within reach. During August 1994, Argentina, Brazil, Paraguay, and Uruguay reached an agreement to establish a customs union on January 1, 1995. A common external tariff was agreed upon for 85 percent of all intraregional tradeable goods. The common external tariff on an additional 10 percent of tradeable goods will be gradually implemented over the next six years. For the remaining 5 percent of tradeable goods, no agreement has yet been reached, and the negotiations have been postponed. It is highly likely that the MERCOSUR will become an imperfect customs union (e.g., with an external tariff agreed upon for approximately 85 percent of all goods traded in the region) by 1995. And if Brazil succeeds in stabilizing its economy in 1994–1995, and Argentina consolidates its program of modernization, regional economic integration may move forward even more rapidly in the future, since the existence of MERCOSUR will probably ease the coordination of trade, exchange-rate, fiscal, credit, and other macroeconomic and sectoral policies.

The first phase of Argentina's liberalization of foreign trade was initiated by the Radical government. Starting in September 1988, the number of tariff items subject to prohibitions or quantitative restrictions was reduced from 4,000 to 3,000, and the average tariff rate was reduced from 51 to 36 percent, although a system of specific tariffs for durable goods and capital goods was retained.

During the second phase, when the BB Plan was in effect and Erman González was economy minister, from

July 1989 to February 1991, the average tariff rate was reduced, to approximately 26 percent at the end of 1989, and 17 percent at the end of 1990. The measures implemented by González also caused a sharp drop in the dispersion of tariffs (a statistical measure of the distribution of tariffs in terms of the average tariff), which fell from nearly 60 percent in mid-1989 to 31 percent by December 1990. Furthermore, a major reduction of specific (fixed amount) tariffs—which had actually constituted the principal obstacle to imports—was instituted.

The third phase was implemented by Economy Minister Cavallo at the beginning of 1991. A graded tariff schedule was introduced, with zero tariffs on raw materials (at the end of 1991 this went up to 5 percent), an 11 percent tariff on intermediate inputs, and a 22 percent tariff on finished manufactured goods. This new graded tariff schedule increased the "rate of effective protection"[16] on goods with the greatest amount of industrial value added. It simultaneously eliminated all remaining specific fees and replaced them with an ad valorem tariff of 22 percent. As a result of this reform, the average tariff rate fell to 10 percent, but the dispersion of tariffs increased considerably, to almost 100 percent.

Only in the automotive and electronic sectors, and for certain used products, such as clothes, motorcycles, and tires, have quotas on imports been maintained. In the case of motor vehicles, a system of quotas has been introduced as part of a sectoral agreement between the government, the automotive companies, and auto parts firms. This agreement is closely related to a bilateral agreement between Argentina and Brazil that provides for greater integration of production between the automotive industries of the two countries within the framework of MERCOSUR.

Imports are subject to a statistical fee in addition to tariffs, which was raised from 3 to 10 percent in October 1992, supposedly in order to reduce the large increase in imports, particularly from Brazil, in the second half of 1992. During 1993, the statistical fee was eliminated for capital goods and significantly reduced for intermediate goods. Under the MERCOSUR agreements, the statistical fee will be eliminated at the end of 1994.

The government also made a serious effort in 1992 to eliminate some of the many administrative obstacles that hampered foreign trade. Many regulations were eliminated; only those connected to health and public safety were kept. All taxes and fees can now be liquidated with a single ticket, and registration requirements for importers and exporters have been simplified.

Argentina repealed its "buy national" law in 1990, and with it went the extraordinary protection national suppliers and contractors enjoyed with respect to government purchasing. The government also eliminated various taxes and other charges on exports, along with restrictions on agricultural exports, except on certain oleaginous products and untreated leather, which the government maintained in the face of pressure from the processed vegetable oil and leatherworking lobbies.

The complex and scarcely effective system of subsidies for exports[17] that prevailed in the 1980s has been eliminated, with the exception of subsidies for products exported from Patagonian ports and the promotional subsidy arrangements for Tierra del Fuego. The former export-promotion system was replaced with a single instrument, an export reimbursement or drawback that varies between 12.5 and 15 percent of the value of the product, depending on estimated indirect taxes on the production costs for each product. Furthermore, mechanisms for refunding domestic value-added taxes paid by exporters have been implemented.

Finally, the government implemented measures at the end of 1992 and during 1993 to increase drawbacks on certain exports of agricultural origin, and drawbacks were granted for the first time for certain traditional products, such as flour and processed rice. Programs to promote exports from the steel, metalworks, capital goods, and farming machinery sectors were launched in 1993. These sectoral programs reduce tariffs on inputs for those companies that can demonstrate convincingly that they are increasing their exports. In early 1994, a government program was launched to encourage industrial specialization and promote exports.

In response to actions initiated by the private sector, the government initiated anti-dumping measures (higher tariffs and/or quotas) in 1993 in the paper, textile, petrochemical, and steel sectors, among others. In addition, the government invoked the MERCOSUR safeguard clause against Brazil with respect to the paper industry and the GATT safeguard clause against imports of milk products from Europe. According to the Ministry of Economy, during the first half of 1994, the average tariff rate plus statistical fee was about 15 percent.

Imports of consumer goods and motor vehicles registered the greatest increase of all imports between 1988 and 1993. Their share of total imports went from 4.5 percent to 26 percent. Imports of capital goods and spare parts have grown at an annual rate of nearly 37.6 percent, increasing in value from $1.4 billion in 1988 to $6.9 billion in 1993 and estimated $9.9 billion in 1994.

The total value of exports increased by 35 percent between 1989 and 1993. Nevertheless, an analysis of international prices for the products Argentina exports and imports shows that the country suffered a deteriora-

TABLE 13. BREAKDOWN OF THE BALANCE OF TRADE (1988–1993) (IN CURRENT DOLLARS)

	1988	1989	1990	1991	1992	1993
TOTAL EXPORTS	9133	9573	12354	11978	12235	13117
Primary Products	2421	2081	3486	3301	3500	3272
Manufactures of Agricultural Origin	3949	4836	4682	4972	4830	4955
Manufactures of Industrial Origin	2624	3160	3348	2938	2823	4665
Fuels/Lubricants	139	296	838	767	1082	1224
TOTAL IMPORTS	5322	4199	4079	8275	14872	16783
Consumer Goods	240	192	255	1514	3205	3527
Motor Vehicles—	—	—	—	202	793	849
Raw and Intermediate Materials	3193	2583	2546	3435	4772	5097
Capital Goods/ Spare Parts	1400	1061	956	2672	5686	6924
Fuels/Lubricants	489	364	322	452	416	386
TRADE BALANCE	3811	5374	8275	3703	-2637	-3666

Source: Instituto Nacional de Estadísticas y Censos, *Boletín del Comercio Exterior Argentino* (1988–1994).

tion in its terms of trade, which fell from 100 in the base year 1986, to 91 for 1990–1992 (see table 5 in the appendix). This is explained by the drop in prices for industrial and agricultural commodities, which constitute a very large portion of Argentina's exports.

However, exports are beginning to pick up. Total exports increased by 7.0 percent in 1993, and are estimated to have grown approximately 18 percent during 1994. Industrial exports, a more relevant indicator of structural change, increased by a dramatic 33.6 percent in 1993 and 30 percent during the first eight months of 1994. Various independent studies have confirmed that the "anti-trade bias,"[18] which measures the incentives to sell in the domestic market as opposed to the foreign market, has significantly improved in the last four years. In addition, due to increases in the prices of commodities, Argentina's terms of trade began to improve during the second semester of 1993.

Studies prepared by the government confirm that reforms have significantly reduced overall levels of effective protection of the protected sectors. The introduction of a tariff schedule graded by value added has substantially reduced the effective protection of such primary sectors as agriculture and food. However, effective protection of intermediate industrial products, such as petrochemicals, glass, cement, steel, containers, thread, wood, and paper, has been only marginally reduced, whereas effective protection of durable goods, capital goods, and other finished products has increased.

In the medium term, the reduction in Argentina's anti-trade bias will bring about structural changes and the reallocation of existing resources, encouraging new investment in export-oriented products. But this process is only now beginning on a significant scale. The memory of the high volatility of real exchange rates and of the acute economic instability of recent decades has slowed the restructuring of the private sector toward greater export orientation. Development of the export sector will take time, new investment, and a major entrepreneurial effort aimed at opening new markets.

The recent increases in drawbacks, the increase in the statistical fee, the announcement of sectoral programs to promote exports, and the anti-dumping and safeguard measures all indicate that the government recognizes that a significant increase in exports will take time. But it has had to make expedient—and, one hopes, temporary—concessions to sectors having difficulties making adjustments. These concessions reduce the probability that such sectors will bring pressures to bear on the general direction of the policy of liberalization, thereby giving reform a better chance to consolidate.

Chapter 4

PROSPECTS FOR ECONOMIC CONVERGENCE

In this chapter, we will first examine the problems of transition faced by Argentina's new economic regime. Then we will turn to the main challenges that Argentina must face if it is to rejoin the group of most advanced countries.

In order for Argentina to once again be counted among this group, its GDP must grow at an annual average rate of 6.5 percent (or 5.3 percent in terms of per capita GDP), during the 25-year period beginning in 1991. If it does so, in 2015, Argentina's per capita GDP will be approximately $21,700, or about 68.5 percent of the projected average GDP ($31,800) for the three most advanced nations. Its standard of living would then correspond to that of Denmark, France, Great Britain, the Netherlands, Italy, and Japan in relation to the three most advanced nations at present, the United States, Canada, and Switzerland. (To perform this calculation we assumed that in 1990 Argentina's per capita GDP was $5,600 and represented an average of approximately 28 percent of the GDP of the three most advanced nations [$20,000], and that the nations in question, already functioning on the technological frontier, would continue to grow during the next 25 years at an average rate of 2 percent per capita, which is consistent with the historical performances of countries in the technological vanguard.) This process of convergence would demand rates of fixed investment and savings on the order of 25 to 28 percent of GDP and a total capital-output coefficient (the capital investment required to produce a unit of output) ranging from 2.5 to 3 (the average capital-output coefficient in Argentina in the 1970s and 1980s was 4.5— see table 3 in the appendix).

The effort required to reach such targets for investment and savings and simultaneously reduce the capital-output coefficient (by improving efficiency and resource allocation) will be very great indeed. Nevertheless, such targets are reachable if the country reorganizes its economic system and completes the process of institutional transformation currently in progress. With the consolidation of the democratic system and the accelerated process of economic reform underway, Argentina is laying the foundations for the resumption of rapid growth.

DIFFICULTIES OF THE TRANSITION

One of the characteristics of the economic restructuring Argentina is undergoing is the existence of imbalances that have the potential to inhibit growth. In terms of Argentina's economic reforms, a number of economic variables are distorted, or are perceived to be distorted, by some economic actors. The most relevant appear to be the delays in the reallocation of resources (capital and labor), high real interest rates, the low rate of domestic savings, and the rise of the real rate of exchange and its corollary, a potential slow growth of exports.

It is important to note that these distortions have characterized the reform process of every developing economy to have successfully implemented major structural reforms, including Chile, South Korea, and Mexico. Striking instances of such occurrences could even have been found in the economies of western Europe and Japan during their economic ¬nd institutional transformations in the immediate postwar period. Furthermore, economies recovering from hyperinflation are liable to undergo some distortions for a relatively prolonged period of time. Unfortunately, if the public and the leadership do not perceive the transitory nature of these imbalances, or if the government responds with inappropriate policies, severe economic and political disturbances can occur, endangering the success of the overall reform program.

A stagnant economy such as Argentina's, having become accustomed over the course of decades to the extreme volatility of key economic variables, has a low propensity to transfer real resources quickly and decisively. Typically, in a stagnant economy, investors concentrate on short-term prospects, firms postpone the launching of new products or the restructuring of operations, employees lose motivation and dedication to the job, and professional training is deferred or its quality decays noticeably. All these perverse phenomena have characterized Argentina's economy in recent decades.

The painful memory of the acute political and economic instability and the permanent disposition to discretionary action that have characterized Argentina's policies in recent decades has led the country's business sector to delay the conversion of the private sector and to postpone decisions to restructure and/or invest in ways that would increase the economy's average productivity. There has been abundant experience internationally, particularly in Germany, South Korea, and Japan, demonstrating that the process of growth and assimilation of technology is not exclusively a technical problem.[1] A successful capitalist system geared toward growth requires a transformation of entrepreneurial energies. "Adventure capitalism," geared primarily to speculation and the practice of securing sinecures and privileges from the government, must be replaced by "innovative capitalism," in which the business community is transformed into the principal vehicle for the assimilation of new technologies.

The transformation of "speculative finance capital" into "productive capital," stimulated by macroeconomic stability and greater levels of certainty, is already occurring in Argentina. An economic and institutional environment that is beginning to favor the profitability of productive activities is reducing the profitability of speculative dealings and increasing the risk for the sinecure businesses that have plagued the modern Argentine economy. The creation of a better-organized government, a strong and independent judiciary, and the curbing of discretionary governmental action should gradually contribute to this process in the coming years.

The slow implementation of labor deregulation, which is still in its early stages, has delayed and complicated the process of resource reallocation in labor-intensive sectors, especially with respect to small and medium-sized firms that operate—or at least would like to operate—in the formal economy. Over-regulation of labor reduces the demand for work, and this keeps rates of unemployment and underemployment at unnecessarily high levels—10.8 percent and 10.2 percent, respectively, as of mid-1994. These high levels of joblessness, in turn, are delaying the staff reductions and administrative reform in provincial governments, where there is an acute surplus of public employees. In other words, Argentina is confronted by a perverse circular effect whereby management postpones hiring new personnel because of the rigidity of current labor contracts, while provincial governments refuse to cut surplus employment for fear of the social consequences of an increase in unemployment.

Limited access to financing and high real interest rates have also delayed resource reallocation. Onerous financing terms have given many business people an excuse to postpone investment and/or reconversion decisions and have lengthened the time frames of productive transformations needed to increase productivity.

Growth requires an array of apparently contradictory interest-rate conditions to be fulfilled simultaneously. The reform program's success demands the maintenance of tight monetary policies and high interest rates to consolidate stability, promote remonetization, and encourage an increase in domestic savings. Growth, on the other hand, benefits from low interest rates and easily available funds, preferably obtainable on a long-term basis, to facilitate risk-taking and provide business sectors with incentives to invest.

Big businesses have recovered access to short-term credit (less than a year) in pesos and "argendollars" (i.e., placements of dollars in the domestic financial market), and they have benefited from the strong recovery of credit relating to foreign-trade operations (i.e., letters of credit, pre-financing of exports). Their access to long-term financing is still limited, as confirmed by the rapidly increasing but still modest amount of corporate debt and equity issues placed in 1992, 1993, and 1994, and the relatively short-term basis on which the local banking sector is still operating. Small and medium-sized firms only have access to short-term credit, often on expensive terms. The government is trying to set up lines of medium-term financing for this sector, but it is still too soon to try to evaluate the results of such efforts.

Obviously, the increase in the financial sector's lending ability in the future will depend on the economy's rate of remonetization and the average level of legal reserve requirements against deposits in the domestic financial system. In international terms, current average levels of central bank required banking cash reserves are high (25 percent as of June 30, 1994), but they should fall gradually in the future. The government is afraid to reduce cash reserve requirements, however, because of the effects an expansion of domestic credit might have on aggregate demand. Here the government is facing a tough short-term dilemma. Productive conversion of the private sector, especially of small and medium-sized firms, requires increasing access to credit, but expansion of credit can weaken stabilization efforts and ignite inflation.

During this stage of economic reform, the government has its hands tied. It is attempting to improve the private sector's access to credit, however, by maintaining a sufficient fiscal surplus so as to limit as much as possible its borrowing in the financial markets and thus avoid using up scarce available credit; negotiating credit lines with international agencies that could be oriented toward providing long-term credit to the local private sector; and rewriting the bankruptcy laws to enhance the collectibility of credit granted, reduce risks for creditors, and provide incentives for making more credit available on more attractive terms to lesser-known small and medium-sized firms.

The conflict will be resolved gradually in the medium term. Progress in remonetization, the gradual reduction of cash-reserve requirements for banks, and the full integration of the domestic capital market into the international market will make credit more accessible and gradually reduce real interest rates to international levels, reduce brokerage fees, and progressively increase access to credit on more favorable terms.

Current levels of national savings appear to be insufficient to sustain rapid growth over the long term. From 1970 to 1988, the levels of total savings were relatively high, fluctuating between 17 and 25 percent of GDP. Unfortunately, a growing portion of these savings was channeled into "defensive" investments abroad, real estate (such as summer or weekend houses around Buenos Aires and in Mar del Plata and Punta del Este), and investments of low economic productivity—the result of the severe distortions that beset the Argentine economy at the time.

In the last two decades, operating fiscal deficits, service payments on the foreign debt (which rose sharply after 1981), and ambitious government investment programs (which represented about 8 percent of GDP up until the crisis of 1982 and then fell to an average annual rate of 3 to 4 percent of GDP thereafter) left the government with large and growing consolidated public-sector deficits. The government financed its programs and deficits from surpluses in the social security system (1970–1975), through foreign savings (1977–1982), through domestic savings mobilized through the placement of public securities, and by raising reserve requirements against deposits in the banking sector and printing money (the inflationary tax).

Between 1977 and 1981, foreign savings fluctuated between 1 and 2 percent of GDP. From the beginning of the foreign debt crisis in 1982 until 1990, average annual foreign savings were slightly negative; however, this marginal negative level does not reflect the real flight of capital since nonvoluntary debt refinancing (mostly ar-

TABLE 14. COMPOSITION OF SAVINGS AS PERCENTAGE
OF GDP (1970–1992)

YEAR	NATIONAL SAVINGS %	FOREIGN SAVINGS[a] %	TOTAL SAVINGS %
1970/79	22.0	1.5	23.5
1980	23.2	1.9	25.1
1981	21.2	1.5	22.7
1982	20.5	−0.5	20.0
1983	20.7	−0.4	20.3
1984	19.9	−0.7	19.2
1985	19.9	−1.8	18.1
1986	16.8	0.6	17.4
1987	17.0	1.8	18.8
1988	19.5	−0.8	18.7
1989	17.8	−2.3	15.5
1990	17.0	−3.0	14.0
1991	14.9	−0.3	14.6
1992	14.0	2.8	16.8
1993	15.7	2.9	18.6

Source: Ministerio de Economía, *Argentina en Crecimiento* (May 1993 and
April 1994).
[a] To calculate foreign savings, the current account deficit of the balance of
payments was adjusted by taking into account an estimate of the
interest and dividends received by Argentine residents on their
foreign-assets holdings, as well as an attempt to discriminate that
portion of the domestic public debt (denominated in foreign currency)
held by foreigners.

rears in interest accrued on unpaid foreign debt) disguised the large capital outflows that occurred during the period.

Between 1989 and 1991, total savings fell substantially, to 14.7 percent of GDP, as a result of capital flight and the drop in per capita income levels and the perverse effects of the inflation tax on the savings capacity of the public. Private-sector savings do not appear to have recovered significantly in the last three years, despite increases in economic activity. This is not surprising, however, in view of the fact that, in 1991, 1992, and 1993, the private sector repatriated a large portion of the funds it had hoarded[2] and invested abroad in recent years. The reduction in levels of risk in the domestic economy and low international interest rates provided the incentives for bringing these funds back into the country, which were used to finance a large part of the increase in spending on durable goods by the private sector.

Economic history shows that the influences on levels of savings and accumulation of wealth are varied and differ not only from one country to another but also over time within the same country. In Argentina's case, once the process of portfolio restructuring has been completed and more of the hoarded funds have been repatriated, it is reasonable to expect that the private sector will again increase its level of savings. It is highly probable that in a setting of greater stability the high rates of private sector savings that characterized the 1970–1982 period (around 20 percent of GDP) will again become the norm. But the motives behind such savings and their composition will probably be very different from what they were in the past. Greater stability will mean that Argentines will not need to hedge against an uncertain future, and they should begin saving to finance a greater rate of investment and/or to raise the social and economic level of their families.

Growth will increase capital's rate of profitability, which will cause a significant increase in retained profits. For firms and entrepreneurs, the new situation will give rise to increases in savings motivated by new investment opportunities. This process, in which the increase of the rate of growth boosts the return on investment and at the same time raises the rate of investment and savings, is characteristic of all economies that have accelerated their growth. Growth will also boost the level of real wages, which will provide incentives for individuals to increase their savings with a view to improving their future living conditions. The possibility of obtaining medium- and long-term credit to buy a house or for purchase of durable goods, as well as the new private pension system, will accelerate this tendency.

To promote and channel savings toward the most productive investments, the domestic capital market must undergo a major institutional transformation. The growth of private pension funds, already underway, must be consolidated, and vigorous, competitive, and solid financial capital markets must be developed. To this end, regulatory agencies, particularly the Superintendency of Banking, the National Securities Commission, and the Insurance Superintendency must strengthen their organizational capacity and substantially improve the quality of their oversight operations to protect the savings the public will increasingly direct toward banks, pension funds, and insurance companies that do business in Argentina.

If Argentina embarks on a process of accelerated growth and convergence, foreign savings (defined as the deficit in the current account) could reasonably contribute an annual average of 3 percent to GDP. (South Korea's average annual deficit in its current account between 1966 and 1985 was 5.2 percent of GDP).[3] Historically, Argentina's annual foreign investment (not exactly comparable to foreign savings, but illustrative nonetheless) on average accounted for somewhat more than 10 percent of GDP in the period of convergence that lasted from 1900 to 1929.[4]

National and foreign private-sector savings should be supplemented by public-sector savings. The government should aim to have a fiscal surplus so that, after servicing the public debt, it can finance its investment program—approximately 4 percent of GDP—from its own resources and generate additional savings of at least 1 percent of GDP, which could be channeled toward the repurchase of the public debt (to the extent that such debt sells in the market at less than its par value) and/or toward long-term financing of small and medium-sized firms.

This will require an increase over the 1993 public sector's fiscal surplus of approximately $3 billion (about 1 percent of GDP). Such an increase in public-sector savings seems feasible if we assume increases in public expenditures in years to come that are less than the rate of GDP growth. There is no mechanism more effective and less painful than this for reducing public spending as a percentage of GDP. If we assume an average GDP growth rate of 6.5 percent for the next ten years, and a growth of public spending of 4.2 percent, public spending will gradually decline, from approximately 28 percent of GDP in 1994, to about 25 percent.

Despite the current low levels in the rate of savings, an Argentine economy launched on a process of accelerated growth would not have insurmountable problems in mobilizing the national and foreign savings necessary to finance the high levels of investment—say, 25 to 28 percent of GDP—that will be necessary to sustain the process of convergence. Such a rate of investment could be financed by private-sector savings on the order of 20 percent of GDP, government savings on the order of 5 percent of GDP, and foreign savings of about 3 percent of GDP.

Of all the transitional difficulties considered thus far, the level of the real exchange rate—the nominal exchange rate adjusted for the effects of domestic and international inflation—is the most complicated issue, and the one that gives rise to the greatest conceptual disagreements and the most heated arguments. The real rate of exchange determines the domestic purchasing power of foreign currencies. It tells us how expensive a country is for other countries and how competitive its economy is in comparative international terms. Among the most important determining factors of the real exchange rate are capital movements, evolution of the terms of trade, trade policy, the level of government spending, and increases in productivity and technological innovation.

In general terms, economists concur in the notion that high volatility in the real rate of exchange—such as characterized Argentina's economy for the past two decades—increases business risk, reduces levels of investment, and places a drag on adjustments in the real economy. Economists are also in general agreement that different real rates of exchange imply different income and profitability levels for the various activities and production factors that make up an economy. In an open economy, the real rate of exchange exerts a significant influence on relative prices for the economy and, thereby, on resource allocation among various activities and on the distribution of income. Very frequently, distortions in the real exchange rate cause an overvaluation of the domestic currency, which is damaging to the profitability of internationally marketable goods (also called tradeable goods) and, with the passage of time, may provoke a balance-of-payments crisis.

In recent years, reference has been made in the economic literature to the need for maintaining an adequate, or "equilibrium," real rate of exchange, one that would make it possible to take advantage of the opportunities available through international trade and at the same time attract foreign investment and generate rapid growth in the domestic economy without having the economy fall into a balance-of-payments crisis. Although the idea is eminently sensible, the difficulty lies in determining precisely what constitutes the equilibrium level for the real exchange rate over the long term. To complicate things still further, various empirical studies have confirmed that countries that grow rapidly and increase their productivity have observed a decline (or overvaluation) in their real exchange rates.

It is hard to determine what would be the appropriate real exchange rate over the long term for an economy such as Argentina's, which is coming out of a hyperinflationary period and undergoing a process of profound structural reform that entails major reallocations of resources and substantial increases in the productivity levels of domestic capital and labor. Undoubtedly, the reform process under way should generate a real exchange rate substantially lower than the average equilibrium real exchange rate of the last twenty years.

Similarly, it is also reasonable to expect that Argentina's economy, once launched on a process of convergence and high growth, should tolerate substantial deficits in the current account for extended periods. This was the Argentine experience during the 1870–1929 period of high growth and convergence and was also characteristic of a number of the more successful economies in the postwar period. It is natural that an open economy with high growth potential should attract foreign capital, and that such capital should contribute to increased rates of domestic savings and should be a preferred vehicle for technology transfer. The sustainability of such a deficit in the current account would depend fundamentally on investors' confidence in Argentina, the country's fiscal and growth performance, and the ratio of Argentina's external liabilities to GDP.

The following additional conditions would make such current account deficits manageable over time: if the inflow of capital is primarily from the private sector to finance increases in the level of investment; if exports grow rapidly, thereby sending a message to international capital markets that an extensive and successful reallocation of resources is under way; and if the government maintains a budget surplus and thus remains independent of foreign financing to settle its fiscal accounts. An effective policy of banking oversight and regulation to limit the vulnerability of the financial sector when sudden capital movements take place will also be necessary.

In recent months, numerous voices in Argentina have raised an alarm about the overvalued peso or the declining value of the dollar. In fact, the real exchange rate in the last three years has been revalued substantially, whether it is measured in dollars or against a "currency basket," or whether it is adjusted for the effects of changes in trade policy, such as export refunds or import tariffs. At the same time, the increase in average wages in dollars has not produced a corresponding increase in the index of the purchasing power of wages (see table 4 in the appendix). Finally, relative prices have gone up for private services—in particular, for education, health, and housing—and down for internationally marketable goods—notably for industrial, agricultural, and food products.

It is argued that this currency revaluation could erode confidence in the Convertibility Plan, induce business people to defer or direct their investments toward the production of goods that are not internationally marketable—and therefore not exposed to competition with foreign imports—and that over time it could cause a severe currency-exchange crisis that would upset the reform program.

From an overall macroeconomic point of view, the situation as of September 1994 does not resemble such a scenario. The central bank has voluminous international reserves backing the monetary base. The government's fiscal performance is relatively solid. The government has a slight budget deficit and has stabilized the stock of public debt. The large capital inflow of the past three years has not been used to finance government expenditures, nor has the government granted explicit or implicit guarantees concerning private-sector indebtedness, and practically all the outstanding government debt is long term.

The deficits in the current account for 1991, 1992, and 1993 essentially represented a process of capital repatriation and increased private-sector indebtedness, which was balanced by an increase in holdings of domestic currency and a large increase of working capital and physical investment by the private sector, in addition to having marginally financed certain increases in spending on durable goods.

The private-sector indebtedness that is the underlying element in the current-account deficit does not represent a significant change in the position of private-sector wealth, but rather a modification of its composition. As initial levels of indebtedness for the private sector, in particular for the domestic banking sector, were very low at the beginning of the stabilization program, it seems highly improbable that the economy will be facing a private-sector liquidity or solvency crisis in the immediate future. It is highly likely that, in the near term, Argentina's capital inflow will stay at relatively high levels, since there is still a large amount of Argentine funds to be repatriated, the process of privatization will continue through 1995, and the implementation of the Brady Plan during 1993 augmented the flow of international financing available to Argentina in the near future.

It is easier to understand what happened to real exchange rates if we recall that, by mid-1989, Argentines had hoarded $45–50 billion in foreign liquid assets. Gradually, starting in 1990, Argentines began to rebalance their portfolio of liquid assets, increasing their demand for domestic currency and other assets located inside the country. At the same time, investment opportunities generated by economic restructuring and privatizations have attracted a large amount of additional direct foreign investment, which has helped to increase the value of domestic assets and, indirectly, to revalue the peso. Similarly, the process of reestablishing foreign credit for foreign trade activities accelerated during the course of 1991, 1992, and 1993 and has generated a large capital inflow.

Under these circumstances, during the first phase of the stabilization plan, the revaluation of the peso and other domestic assets is a phenomenon that cannot be curbed, and there is little the government can do in the way of fiscal or monetary policy to put off a recovery of the local currency, which basically reflects a restoration of confidence in the domestic economy and a reestablishment of international credit at levels considered normal. Although other economies, such as Chile's, have successfully implemented efficient control mechanisms on the entry of capital, such mechanisms would have little capacity to limit or control capital movements in a country as "dollarized" as Argentina. In principle, the current exchange rate seems sustainable so long as the government maintains fiscal balance and continues reducing the inflation rate, and so long as there is no increase of uncertainty in the approaching electoral season.

Nevertheless there is still worry in the air about the effects a possible peso overvaluation may have on productive resource allocation and on Argentina's capacity to create a dynamic export sector, which is pivotal to an accelerated process of reintegration of Argentina's economy with the international economy. In the past, Argentina has not been able to combine GDP growth with the development of exports, and this experience gives rise to doubts about the future.

In addition, doubts have been raised recently about the sustainability of the Convertibility Plan after the May 1995 presidential and general elections. The significant changes which have occurred in the international capital markets since February 1994, resulting from the increases in short- and long-term dollar interest rates, have produced a modest slowdown in foreign capital inflows into Argentina. While trade financing remains strong, capital market financing has become more volatile, more expensive, and final maturities for the issuance of debt have shortened. Also, the public foreign debt interest service is beginning to increase, imposing a heavier burden on the government's fiscal resources.

The annual rate of remonetization of the economy (measured as M3 plus local dollar deposits) has declined from 130 percent in 1991, to 63 percent in 1992, to 48 percent in 1993, and is expected to grow at 25 percent during 1994. Also the country risk premium, which had declined to 4.2 percent in 1993, increased to 5.6 percent during the first nine months of 1994. The trade deficit has continued to increase and will probably reach close to $5.8 billion in 1994. However, exports—particularly industrial exports—are growing rapidly, and it is possible that increases occurring in international commodity prices, as well as the recent stabilization of the Brazilian economy, might gradually improve the terms of trade for Argentina, and the trade deficit may stabilize or even decline during 1995.

Although the economy continues to grow rapidly, unemployment increased from 8.8 percent in May 1993 to 10.2 percent in May 1994. Finally, the fiscal equilibrium reached in 1993 has deteriorated in 1994, and there are fears that this trend might worsen in 1995. The deterioration of the fiscal performance is the result of a program initiated by the government at the end of 1993 to compensate the local business sector for its high operating costs with tax reductions. A policy of gradually reducing the employers' contributions to the social security system was introduced in 1994 for the industrial, agriculture, construction and mining sectors, and the government intends to extend these benefits to all remaining sectors in the economy in 1995. In addition, as a result of the implementation of the new private pension system, a substantial portion of the amounts previously raised to fund the government's pension system have been transferred to the new private pension funds.

Finally, the provincial governments' public finances are not balanced, and the ability of the national government to encourage a major fiscal restructuring is limited by the electoral season, which has already begun and will last until mid-1995. In the meantime, tax collection efforts during the first nine months of 1994 have not increased at the rate projected by the government.

The federal government has announced its intention to reduce its total expenditures by about 5 percent and to increase its revenue, not by increasing tax rates, but through a major reduction in tax evasion in the areas of the value-added tax, income tax, and social security contributions (the government estimates that approximately four and a half million workers are not registered in the social security system). The increase in the dollar interest rates and the slowdown in the remonetization process will reduce the credit expansion that occurred during the last three years, and a contraction in economic activity might reduce tax revenues further and aggravate the still-modest deterioration in the fiscal performance.

Despite these negative trends, the Convertibility Plan will probably be maintained. The fear of instability is strong in the local population, and Argentina has ample experience proving that nominal devaluations have not succeeded in introducing the needed structural changes nor in stabilizing the economy. For political reasons, the government will not encourage a devaluation and hopes that, if President Menem is reelected in 1995, a second wave of structural reforms and greater international and domestic confidence will allow the local economy to increase its productivity as a result of the major resource reallocation and increased levels of investment now underway.

This does not automatically mean that Argentina's fixed exchange parity will last forever. Argentina is far from the major international markets and agricultural and industrial commodities will probably remain, at least in the near future, an important component of its exports. In other words, Argentina's economy might be subject to major fluctuations originating abroad, and a fixed exchange rate might seriously limit its ability to adjust to external shocks that might require a devaluation or revaluation of its currency. However, the memory of the instability of the last twenty years and the 1989–1990 hyperinflation provide a psychological and political anchor that will not be easily removed except by a fundamental change in domestic circumstances, or a major external shock.

THE CHALLENGE OF SUSTAINED GROWTH

The necessary annual growth rate for reaching convergence—6.5 percent of GDP—may seem high compared to Argentina's historical performance. Nonetheless, the Argentine economy has the potential to reach and sustain such growth rates for a prolonged period of time. Nations as diverse as Germany, Italy, Brazil, China, South Korea, Japan, Singapore, and Taiwan have seen their GDP and per capita income grow at rates higher than 6.5 percent and 5.3 percent, respectively, for extended periods of time. Argentina shares more of the characteristics of an obsolete economy than those of an underdeveloped economy. It will probably need a fairly prolonged period of accelerated technological and productivity growth in order to catch up.

However, to grow rapidly in the years to come, Argentina will simultaneously have to strengthen market mechanisms and the government's organizational capability. The interplay of forces between society, markets, and the government does not have to be a zero-sum game. In the present historical circumstances, to maximize the society's potential for progress, it will be necessary to bring about an increase in the power and efficiency of both markets and the government.

The stagnation and isolation of the last twenty years left Argentina with a technologically obsolete stock of physical capital, and it lags in the assimilation of advanced scientific and technological knowledge. But this "technology gap" represents a unique opportunity for Argentina to rapidly assimilate available technologies at the international level, take advantage of economies of scale and specialization, and quickly raise the average productivity of the domestic economy.

There are already palpable signs that economic restructuring seems to be proceeding in the right direction. Reform is beginning to raise levels of productivity for labor and capital through a gradual process of resource reallocation and recovery of investment levels. Economic growth in the last four years has been substantial (GDP increased by approximately 32 percent). Most private sector forecasts project a cooling of the economy in 1995 and a GDP increase of around 4.5 percent in 1994.

Although the initial expansion was caused by a greater utilization of installed productive capacity that had been idle in recent years, it is indisputable that a growing portion of the increases in productivity are coming from new investment and reallocation of productive resources. Investment levels are still very low but, in current dollars, they increased by 70 percent between 1989 and 1993. Most of the increase was the result of private-sector investment. Private investment has been geared principally to productive consolidation of recently privatized enterprises, the construction sector, the oil and natural gas sectors, wholesale and retail trade, the service sector (hotels, restaurants, education, and health), and defensive investments in sectors producing internationally marketable goods.

Imports of capital goods, such as machinery and spare parts, have increased dramatically from approximately $1 billion per year for 1989–1990, to an estimated $9.9 billion (almost 3.6 percent of GDP) for 1994. Utilization of installed capacity for the domestic capital goods industry and domestic production of heavy utility vehicles have increased by 25 percent and 100 percent, respectively, since April 1991. Consumption of cement, consumption of rolled steel, and construction permits issued in the federal capital since the beginning of the Convertibility Plan have increased 65 percent, 55 percent, and 75 percent, respectively, as of August 1994.

Public support for the democratic regime, as well as the solid support for the system's legitimacy, is slowly reducing the levels of political uncertainty that have characterized contemporary Argentina. With the passage of time, the continuation of this process will help to increase confidence levels among domestic and foreign investors, which will boost the rate of capital accumulation and redirect investment toward projects that take longer to reach fruition and have a greater potential long-term return on investment.

The average educational levels of the population seem to be more than sufficient for the first steps toward assimilating new technology into the domestic economy. (One of Argentina's problems has been the underutilization of skilled human resources—engineers working as technicians, technicians who work in jobs that do not require technical training.) The sharp drop in personal income and the suffering occasioned by the last twenty years of instability are motivating people to make an additional effort to improve their standard of living. Increases in the number of hours worked, in the percentage of the population that wants to work (see table 4 in the appendix), and in enrollment in institutions offering vocational training and adult education are unmistakable signs of the change in expectations taking place among broad sectors of the population.

In the private sector, reforms are helping to increase levels of competition and pressuring the domestic and foreign business sectors to restructure their operations, reduce their costs, and increase their investment to improve their products. The processes of trade liberalization and deregulation have accelerated since 1991. Imports increased from $4.1 billion in 1990, to $16.8 billion in 1993, which has put pressure on the profit margins of producers of goods that compete with imports but has also reduced the costs to producers using imported goods, improving their competitiveness. Deregulation in such key sectors as transportation, ports, and domestic trade is beginning to have similar effects, reducing profit margins for those sectors but increasing the benefits for users in the more competitive environment.

The strengthening of public finances and, in particular, the gradual reduction of tax evasion and the elimination of numerous tax loopholes, subsidies, and regional and sectoral promotion schemes is reducing serious price distortions in factors of production and in goods and services, which had seriously penalized economic efficiency and distorted investment flows.

Privatizations are profoundly altering the country's economic structure. The vast economic power that until recently was concentrated in the hands of the state has been decentralized and distributed among a fairly large group of new domestic and foreign private firms. The privatizations are bringing about a transfer of real assets, as well as underutilized and poorly managed human resources, to private firms, which are significantly improving their productivity. In certain areas, such as oil and railroads, privatizations will increase levels of competition, and in all privatized companies a series of new business opportunities are being opened up to suppliers and users. Furthermore, the new private companies will promote the assimilation of technological innovation, which will have a positive effect on the quality of goods and services produced.

The process of reform is also forcing the public sector at the national and provincial levels to face two big problems that were well known, although they had been obscured by the high inflation and instability of recent decades: the deficient organizational ability of the state apparatus, which resulted in the low quality and low efficiency of public expenditures, and the high levels of taxation resulting from the acute disparities between taxpayers who pay their taxes and those who evade them.

Direct foreign investors are becoming involved in Argentina in large numbers. Between 1990 and 1993, foreign investors invested at least $10 billion in the country. This amount of direct foreign investment more than doubles the total stock of direct foreign investment made in Argentina up to 1989.[5] Most foreign direct investment during 1991–1993 was related to the privatization of government enterprises. In 1994, a substantial and growing flow of foreign direct investment began occurring in the automobile and food industries as well as in the mining and oil gas sectors, and in private services (insurance, banking, distribution).

Conditions in the Southern Cone (Argentina, Brazil, Chile, Paraguay, and Uruguay) are, for the first time in decades, favorable to a process of regional integration. Changes of economic policy that have already been put into place in Chile and are beginning to be made in Brazil are laying the basis for strengthening their respective private sectors, promoting international trade, and liberalizing the region's domestic economies. For the first time in 60 years, these reforms are creating a favorable framework for the growth of genuine regional integration.

The attempt to create a free trade zone and customs union between Argentina, Brazil, Paraguay, and Uruguay (MERCOSUR) continues to move forward, a program of tariff elimination is being carried out, and despite various difficulties, Argentine-Brazilian cooperation is growing. Between 1988 and 1993, Argentina's total trade with the MERCOSUR countries increased dramatically, from $2 billion in 1988, to $6.4 billion in 1993. Total bilateral trade between Argentina and Chile also increased rapidly, from $410 million in 1988, to $1.3 billion in 1993. In September 1994, Chile and the MERCOSUR countries initiated negotiations toward the creation of a free trade zone and the possible incorporation of Chile into MERCOSUR at a later date.

Direct foreign investment flows are also growing significantly within the region; during the last three years Chileans have invested more than $1 billion in Argentina alone. Various large projects of regional integration under the leadership of the private sector involving transportation, natural gas, and oil are underway or in the final stages of negotiation.

The significant increase in investment levels, the repatriation of capital, and the new wave of direct foreign investment are the most obvious signs that the reform of the Argentine economy is making headway. Nevertheless, what has been achieved to date is not enough if Argentina intends to accelerate its economic growth. To consolidate its new economic regime, Argentina will also have to reconstruct its governmental organization at both the national and provincial levels, radically transform its educational system, and further integrate its economy with the international economy.

Reconstruction of the Government

A well-organized government with an efficient bureaucracy does not by itself guarantee growth and cannot take the place of functioning markets. Growth fundamentally depends on private initiative, entrepreneurial creativity and innovation, and the ability, training, and motivation of a country's people. Nevertheless, a well-organized government is a necessary condition for accelerated growth. Governments cannot create competitive industries, but they can create an economic and social climate in which they can flourish.

Through spending on education, health care, and infrastructure, governments can improve the quantity and the quality of domestic production factors. Similarly, policies that stimulate competition, encourage innovation, and facilitate more productive activities promote growth. The quality of any government fundamentally depends on its organizational capacity, which, in turn, depends on the quality, stability, and loyalty of its public officials.

The twenty economically most advanced countries (see table 3) all combine established democratic systems, market economies, and relatively well-organized government structures with a certain degree of autonomy and independence with respect to the rest of society. Governments can compile in a timely fashion the statistical data needed to evaluate the society's social and economic situation; monitoring their own efficiency and competence; set up procedures to improve performance and plan for the medium term; supervise the workings of the economy, and regulate such essential areas as health, public safety, the environment, prices for public services, and public savings; and generally execute the functions society has delegated to them and administer their expenditures with as much efficiency and probity as possible.

To be sure, the governments of the most advanced countries carry out these immense and varied tasks with varying degrees of effectiveness. The debate on the role and effectiveness of government is a permanent one in the societies in question. But we should not let such controversies obscure the underlying issue: the advanced countries and those growing rapidly all have relatively effective and well-organized governments. Among the follower countries who have managed to catch up with the most advanced nations, or whose growth rates have accelerated rapidly in recent decades, there is also a fairly strict correlation between the quality and organizational capability of the government and economic convergence.

In chapter 2, we looked at the serious organizational weaknesses of Argentina's government. We observed that the Argentine government was never well organized, that it had always had a limited degree of autonomy, and that it was not able in the course of the twentieth century to organize a professional civil service with a nucleus of well-trained career officials loyal, above all, to the state itself. We noted the patrimonial attitude that has characterized Argentina's government and caused corruption, patronage, and the excessive politicization of its institutions. And we saw how the interventionist state over the past two decades perceptibly exacerbated pre-existing institutional fragility by drastically expanding the government's responsibilities without making concurrent improvements in its organizational capabilities.

In recent decades, Argentina's government, both at the national and provincial levels has existed in a state of permanent crisis. First, there has been a marked deterioration in the efficiency, competence, and equity of public spending. The government apparatus responsible for social spending—which amounted to $47 billion in the 1993 budget—has lost its ability to function and, in general, the effects of its policies on the efficiency of the economy as a whole are not known. The quality of goods and services the government provides to society is generally very low. Its competence as a regulator of the public health and safety, the environment, and economic competition was never very high to begin with, and has fallen to truly disturbing levels in recent decades.

Second, Argentina suffers from its lack of a professional civil service. The main technical and administrative positions are usually occupied by political appointees. It is customary for each new minister, secretary of state, provincial governor, or head of a public enterprise or decentralized agency to bring in his own "crew" to take over the principal administrative positions, along with a large group of advisers to formulate policy. Furthermore, it has been customary in Argentina for political appointees to occupy even very low positions on the bureaucratic ladder. The tradition of a nonprofessional civil service is an old one. In the 1930s the functioning of the Argentine government depended on a few eminent figures, known as "proconsuls," who managed with great autonomy large areas of the government without however institutionalizing public service as a career.

The lack of a professional civil service has led to the excessive concentration of responsibilities in the office of the president and the minister of the economy at the national level. Efforts to make the government work with "all-star teams" brought in from the private sector are symptoms of the same problem and, unfortunately, such teams have been able to provide only temporary solutions to the problem of institutional fragility. The salaries of public officials are well below salaries for comparable positions in the private sector. This has contributed significantly to corruption and in the last ten years has given rise to unpublicized "supplementary payment" schemes by the government in power to assure the loyalty and permanence of high officials. This is a perverse system in that it only applies to certain high officials, and it diminishes their capacity to act with probity and independence in the discharge of their administrative duties.

In recent years, the acute deterioration of governmental organization in Argentina prompted multilateral agencies, mostly through programs of technical assistance financed by the United Nations Development Programme, to propose that the government contract consultants to strengthen key areas of administration. Although the objective was a good one and positive results were achieved in some cases, the solution was at best a temporary fix. In many instances, the monies were used to finance the salaries of the advisers and members of the political entourage of the administration in power, adding to the frustration of career officials who continue to receive lower salaries.

Neither the "brilliant administrators" of the 1930s nor the all-star teams nor the consultants have established a government of competent officials devoted to the country's interests. All such efforts to strengthen public administration from without are doomed to failure. They impede the growth of a class of professional career civil servants, and the continuous changes in personnel give rise to defensive behavior among officials, whose decision-making is driven by concern for job security.

Hyperinflation, the repudiation of the public debt, and the dramatic administrative decay of the governmental apparatus were the final symptoms of the severe crisis that devastated Argentina. The crisis gave rise to a deep lack of confidence in the government. From the mid-1980s to this day, the Argentine public has shown an increasing desire to curb the functions of the government, at the same time demanding better administration of justice, public safety, education, public health, and environmental control.

Reducing the national government's role in the economy (through privatizations), curbing its prerogatives (through deregulation), and focusing its activity more narrowly have been essential first steps in making its relationship with society saner and more productive. The provincial governments are lagging in the process of fiscal and administrative reform, though a few have begun to adjust their budgets, reform their tax systems, promote deregulatory measures, and privatize inefficient enterprises. In most cases the agenda for reform has not been addressed, and necessary improvements are resisted by government employee labor unions and by important segments of local political establishments. Once the reform process and the privatizations in progress have been completed, however, Argentina's national and provincial public sector will still generate approximately 22–25 percent of GDP and will be responsible for public expenditures amounting to between 35 and 40 percent of GDP. In addition, government reform is a prerequisite to improving income distribution and creating a more just society. The national and provincial governments spend about 18 percent of GDP to fulfill their social responsibilities (in public health, education, pensions, and infrastructure investments in poor areas). The lack of an organized government apparatus greatly reduces the effectiveness of these expenditures, penalizing the poorest sectors of society.

The crisis affords Argentina the historic opportunity to reform its government from the bottom up. The success of this effort will depend on the existence of a professional civil service based on merit, substantially free of personal or political favoritism, and with a core of technically qualified officials who are loyal above all to the government. To promote such a civil service, the government will have to institutionalize impartial administrative recruiting procedures, such as anonymous, written entry examinations, and promotion arrangements that ensure the advancement of the most capable officials. Civil servants at the highest professional levels should be immune to removal from their jobs without congressional approval. An in-depth reform of the institutions that train and prepare professional civil servants is also needed. As the experiences of France and Japan reveal, an excellent civil service depends upon intensive and specialized training programs, which foster an esprit de corps that helps to segregate governmental administrators from special interests.

With the creation of a professional civil service based on merit and professional excellence, the political leadership will be able to discharge its most important functions with greater effectiveness and rationality. International experience shows that, in general, career officials are jealous guardians of their own prestige (which is the basis for their future promotions), and the job security they enjoy gives them incentives to protect the interests of the government.

Comprehensive Reform of the Educational System

Recent theories on economic growth accord special importance to education and training. A number of empirical studies have found a strong correlation between a society's stock of human capital, as measured by school enrollment, literacy rates, and cumulative spending on education, and economic growth rates.[6] Education increases the population's capacity to adapt to new technologies, procedures, inputs, and products, and encourages initiative, innovation, and business sense. Economic growth, in turn, increases activities that require highly skilled personnel.

Although education and technical training are indispensable to economic growth, they are not sufficient in themselves to promote it. The countries of eastern Europe made a big effort to develop human resources in the postwar period without achieving sustained increases in productivity or growth. Indeed, one of the common attributes of these societies was the underutilization of highly skilled human resources.

Argentina has also made a relatively large investment in the development of human resources in recent decades (approximately 5 percent of GDP) and also suffers from acute underutilization of human resources. This has resulted in low real return on educational investment, massive emigration of technicians and specialized workers, and general frustration among trained workers who have no place to apply their skills. Argentina's experience, and that of other countries, shows that spending on education and high educational levels are not in themselves enough to compensate for mistaken macroeconomic policies and defective systems of economic organization.

Argentina's spending on education is more or less similar to what the most advanced nations spend in terms of percentages of GDP. The rates of school attendance are nearly 100 percent at the primary level, 50 percent at the secondary level, and appoximately 32 percent at the higher education level (820,000 students are enrolled in institutions of higher learning). But behind these numbers lurk serious weaknesses in the quality of education and the educational system's integration with the productive system. At the primary school level, there is a high percentage of dropouts (between 10 and 15 percent), and many students repeat a year (45 percent do not complete their studies in the allowed seven years). The rate of secondary school attendance is relatively low compared to such countries as Chile (80 percent), Korea (86 percent), and Spain (96 percent). For this reason, the National Congress has just passed a law that progressively extends compulsory school attendance to the first three years of the secondary cycle. Labor regulations governing teachers are very restrictive and have led to an educational establishment resistant to change. The other side of this restrictive labor scheme is very low pay, which undermines the quality of instruction and reduces teachers' motivation.

At the university level, only one out of every ten students graduates, but this is not the result of tough exams and strong competition but of what must be one of the highest dropout rates in the world. The quality of university education is generally poor, and the relationship between students and the universities is wretched. There is no attempt to follow the individual performance of the students, nor is any pressure brought to bear on students who lag behind or receive bad grades. A recent survey conducted at the medical school of the University of Buenos Aires reveals that 70 percent of the graduates do not consider themselves qualified to practice their profession. Fewer than 10 percent of university professors have teaching as their only job, and salaries are extraordinarily low. The reigning assumption, even in a number of the private universities, is that teaching can only be done as a supplement to other professional activities. In sum, the system is expensive, does not encourage excellence either among teachers or students, and often produces mediocre university graduates with mediocre qualifications.

Although Argentina's educational system has serious defects, the country's stock of human resources is nonetheless sufficient to supply the country's needs during the early stages of economic reform and sustained growth. The essential problem with Argentina's educational system is not a lack of resources, but ineffectual management of the available resources.

Although this is not the place for a detailed analysis of the educational system's problems,[7] the general outlines of a solution involve regional decentralization; raising teachers' salaries and at the same time increasing their productivity by doing away with obsolete labor regulations; creating standardized national exams to make it possible to evaluate the quality of the education provided; requiring a minimum of ten years of schooling (the "basic cycle"), and regulating access to higher levels of education so as to identify and reward talent and effort; eliminating open admission to universities and transforming them into centers of excellence; and decreasing dropout rates and the repeating of grades, which raise the costs and reduce the effectiveness of education at all levels.

Beyond the first ten years of study, Argentina should consider developing a "dual" system in which students study and work simultaneously during their last three years of schooling. Such a system has been set up with great success in Germany, Austria, Denmark, and Switzerland. The high competitiveness of these economies has been attributed by many observers to the high productivity and training of their labor forces.[8] In all of these countries, of the students who finish the basic cycle, between 50 and 70 percent seek apprenticeships in business, and if they're accepted, they enter into a program of mutually reinforcing work and study. Typically, apprentices spend three or four days each week at work and one or two days at vocational school. After three years, 90 percent get a professional diploma that gives them the credentials to work in their chosen fields. In Germany, diplomas are given for 400 different professions—hairdresser, bankteller, machine operator, sales person, lab assistant, craftsperson, and paramedic among them. Apprentices receive a paycheck equivalent to about 20 to 25 percent of what a graduate of the system would earn from the companies that train them. The rest of the graduates of the basic cycle continue their secondary studies with the aim of either entering the dual system later on or going on to university.

The dual system is organized by the private sector (through chambers of commerce at the national, regional, and municipal levels) and by local governments, and union participation is possible in certain branches of vocational training. The private sector defines the areas in which it will offer training programs; designs, regulates, and supervises the programs; sets up contracts with apprentices; and defines procedures for exams and requirements for the diploma. The public sector finances the educational portion of these programs and, by the terms of the laws regulating vocational training, oversees the contracts and the training.

The main advantages of this system are that it assures a swift transition from school to work and dramatically reduces levels of unemployment among the young. Furthermore, the education and training provided are highly relevant to the development of the domestic economy and facilitate significant increases in productivity and wages for vast segments of the population. In 1882, Argentina had the foresight to adopt the most revolutionary educational innovation of the times: compulsory primary schooling. Argentina should now consider adopting what may be the best vocational training system for labor.[9]

It is obvious that a reform with these revolutionary characteristics will take time, as well as vigorous and enthusiastic collaboration on the part of the business sector. In the meantime, as an intermediate step, the administration of technical, industrial, agricultural, and trade schools should be transferred to national and local chambers of commerce. This has already happened in Chile, where the Sociedad de Fomento Fabril (the employers' federation) has assumed responsibility for the administration of 30 technical schools. The Chilean government provides the financing and retains the right to supervise the development of the system, while the business sector administers the facilities, appoints teachers and directors, draws up programs of study with total freedom, and organizes jobs for students in the firms associated with the chambers of commerce.

The Export Potential of Argentina's Economy

From the standpoint of long-term growth potential, the main problem of Argentina's foreign sector is not the deficit in the balance of trade or in the current account, but the low degree of integration of the domestic economy with the international economy. The openness coefficient of Argentina's economy during the 1980s was extremely low, averaging only 7 percent. The economic crisis of the 1980s produced high average real exchange rates and relative prices very favorable to sectors producing marketable goods. Despite this, and the major incentives and subsidies granted to exports, the country failed to create a dynamic export sector with a high growth potential. Argentina continues to export traditional agricultural products and a range of industrial and agro-industrial commodities, but it exports virtually no "brand-name" products or any of the specialty products for which international demand has been growing rapidly and over which the exporter has some degree of control in setting prices.

A greater degree of integration in international trade is essential if Argentina is to increase the size of its reduced national market, thereby encouraging the development of economies of scale and specialization that constitute a major factor in economic growth. Over the next 12 years, Argentina must substantially increase its openness coefficient from its current level—about 7.5 percent of GDP in 1993—to at least 15 percent of GDP. This means that Argentina, assuming an average annual GDP growth rate of 6.5 percent, will have to increase exports at an average annual rate of 12.8 percent. Although such a growth rate may seem high, a number of countries, including Germany, Italy, Japan, China, South Korea, Thailand, and Taiwan have reached and surpassed these levels for relatively extended periods over the course of recent decades.

In any case, it is not enough for Argentina to balance its foreign accounts through increased capital inflows or a trade surplus generated by a major recession and/or a crisis of confidence. It must also substantially increase its exports and its participation in the world economy. As I noted earlier, once launched on a process of convergence, Argentina will have to put up with a structural deficit in its current account, but such a deficit can be financed in the long run if growth is sustained and the domestic economy is integrated with the international economy through the accelerated growth of its exports. This process has not yet begun on a significant scale. What explains the slowness of the restructuring of the domestic sector producing internationally marketable goods into a new export profile?

First, the process of trade liberalization is very recent and has taken place in a setting of acute economic

imbalances (from 1989 to 1991) and of sweeping structural reform (from 1991 to 1994) in which new private
investment has been directed first to the acquisition of
undervalued assets—both real and financial—and then
toward sectors in the process of privatization.

Second, stability gave rise to recovery in the levels
of economic activity, increased aggregate domestic demand, and reduced exportable surpluses. As a result,
the exportable surplus of various intermediate industrial
products (e.g., steel, paper, and petrochemicals) was
reduced over the last three years. For example, according to data provided by the Centro de Industriales
Sidarugricos, steel-sector exports fell from 2,200,000
million tons in 1989, to 840,000 million tons in 1992.

Third, export conversion requires the opening of
new markets and new investment in sectors of greater
aggregate value, both in the industrial and agro-industrial sectors. It is unlikely that this profound change of
export profile can be completed quickly, since the sectors that should assume a leadership role generally have
not had significant experience with exports in the past.

Fourth, Argentina's tax system, with its strong historical emphasis on levies that penalized production and
export activities, gave rise to a strong anti-trade bias in
the country's productive profile. Furthermore, the deterioration of the physical and institutional infrastructure
and excessive regulation increased costs for the export
sector. Although it is true that many of these hindrances
are being gradually remedied in the framework of structural reforms analyzed in chapter 3, the positive effects
on resource reallocation are not immediate and will take
a while to make themselves felt.

Under the present circumstances, there is only one
possible route to the dynamic integration of Argentina's
economy with the international economy. This road in-

volves extending the structural reforms under way, increasing investor confidence (diminishing the country risk factor), and curbing the anti-export bias that still characterizes the domestic economy.

During the last twelve months, the government has improved the real exchange rate by gradually reducing a number of taxes that penalize production and give rise to an anti-export bias (in particular the provincial tax on gross income—approximately 1.5 percent of GDP—and some provincial taxes levied on the consumption of energy and natural gas by the productive sector). During the next twelve months, these inefficient taxes should be eliminated. The government is also gradually reducing taxes and social security charges levied on labor to a maximum of 30 percent. Export sectors, which generally operate within the formal economy, are heavily discriminated against by the current system. Furthermore, taxes on labor and other social assistance charges are not reimbursable under the rules of GATT. Export activities are also hampered by tax evasion, which distorts the allocation of resources. Increased inforcement of the tax laws is therefore essential.

The government should also continue its policy of deregulation of transportation, ports, airports, and customs services. Although considerable progress has been made in recent years, much remains to be done. Provincial governments, in particular, should commit themselves to deregulation; excessively bureaucratic and troublesome procedures for small and medium-sized exporting firms should be simplified; and monopolies on the services offered at national airports should be eliminated.

Over the longer term, the real exchange rate could be improved if government spending at the national and provincial levels were reduced so that spending increased less than GDP over the next ten years. As noted earlier, increases in the level of government spending tend to revalue the real rate of exchange through various mechanisms. On one hand, public expenditure is a measure of the fiscal pressure on the private sector and on the producers of internationally tradeable goods. When government spending decreases, taxes are lower, costs are lower, and the real rate of exchange is higher. On the other hand, the government has a greater propensity than the private sector to spend on goods that are not internationally tradeable, which distorts relative prices and penalizes the tradeable-goods sector. Furthermore, the public sector employs approximately 16 percent of the labor force and concentrates a very significant portion of its total spending on wages (approximately 60 percent). A policy aimed at reducing public employment and containing spending would facilitate the transfer of some of the human resources with a low level of productivity in their current occupations to more productive jobs in the private sector, which could improve the profitability of the tradeable-goods sector. A policy of gradual containment of public spending would make it possible to reduce the tax pressure on the private sector over time and help to improve the real exchange rate. In the long term, economic growth should lead to accelerated private investment and flows of foreign trade, somewhat smaller increases in private spending and public investment (that is, for infrastructure and for education, health, justice, and public safety), and the containment of the other components of public spending.

Patience is required, however. No economy can open up world markets all at once, or recreate internationally competitive domestic production overnight. International experience suggests that a period of four to five years is the minimum needed to bring about a clear reorientation of the domestic tradeable-goods sector toward exports. Nonetheless, there is no doubt that Argentina possesses major export potential. The agricultural sector could increase its production and export surplus with unusual rapidity by disseminating technologies already available among the broad group of producers who still have not assimilated them. This process could boost agricultural exports on the order of 2 percent of GDP within a short period.[10] To bring about such an increase, the government will have to provide greater access to long-term credit, reduce distorting taxes (taxes on property, gross income, and energy consumption), amplify deregulatory policies, especially at the provincial level in the transportation sector, and eliminate irksome customs and health requirements. The oil and natural gas sector could transform itself quickly into a major exporter, particularly to Brazil and Chile, and increases could easily amount to more than 2 percent of GDP. The industrial and agro-industrial sectors will face the challenge of conversion in the next few years, becoming fully engaged in a process of assimilating technology and developing economies of scale and specialization. While stability and a fiscal surplus will improve the investment climate, structural reforms—liberalization, deregulation, and increased competition—will radically transform the environment of the industrial sector and provide incentives for profound cultural change in the business community. Moving from the production of basic commodities to the world of specialization and differentiation will require major adjustments in the domestic business culture, which will have to begin to emphasize quality control, design, packaging, the search for new markets, and technological innovation.

Argentina has been industrialized for over a hundred years, its industrial base is not insignificant, and it possesses a large stock of skilled human resources. In the last twenty years, a number of large private national groups with sophisticated organizations, the ability to recruit and train human resources, and modern managerial systems have been created. Argentina possesses a capital-intensive intermediate industrial system producing basic inputs that is competitive by international standards. The stagnation of the domestic economy compelled this sector to develop an export profile over the last fifteen years, which in turn provided incentives for a major and continuing effort to reduce costs and improve the quality of its products.

Improvements in the investment climate and changes in the business culture will favor increased productivity and substantially improve the export sector's competitive profile. The government can help to speed up this process through an industrial policy implemented at two different levels. At a general level, industrial policy should be directed toward increasing competitiveness through deregulation of labor and reduction of social security charges; the reduction of taxes that discriminate against production (taxes on assets, gross income, energy consumption, etc.); deregulation of unnecessary regulations and procedures that hinder production and exports, especially ones that penalize small and medium-sized firms; improving the system for promoting export drawbacks and the rapid return to exporters of fiscal credits related to the valued-added tax; fostering and financing a system of apprenticeship and professional training of the kind described above; gradually reducing financing costs and lengthening credit repayment periods in the domestic market; and encouraging long-term credit to finance exports of capital goods through a mechanism of supplier credit, partly financed by the government and implemented through the domestic banking system.

At the sectoral level, the government should work together with the employers' associations to organize and contribute to the financing of programs promoting trade abroad; negotiate bilateral, regional, and multilateral concessions to improve access to foreign markets for domestic producers; foster the creation and financing of private institutes for technological research and quality control to be governed and administered by the private sector; and identify, swiftly investigate, and take appropriate measures within the framework of GATT regulations against instances of "dumping," or discriminatory export subsidies which negatively affect domestic producers. Regarding improved access to foreign markets, Argentina is a strong supporter of the recently signed GATT agreement (the Uruguay Round). In addition, the formal launching of the MERCOSUR customs union in January 1995 and the strong interest shown by government and opposition parties toward the possibility of negotiating free trade zones with NAFTA and the European Union are clear indications of Argentina's international trade policy during the next decade.

The development of a new industrial sector geared to exports will require entrepreneurial effort and investment in products, processes, and new technologies that will bear fruit slowly. It will also require government support for trade promotion and trade negotiations to broaden access to markets. Although the industrial and agro-industrial sectors are the ones facing the greatest challenge, they will be the ones to reap the greatest benefits from the Argentine economy's integration with the international economy. It is possible to imagine an Argentina that, at the end of this conversion process, no longer exports steel wire, aluminum, and pulp, but high-grade specialty steel, aluminum products, and books.

In order to set its "engine of growth" in motion toward sustained and rapid growth in the years to come, Argentina will have to strengthen the role of markets and private activity; reconstruct a government that is effective, autonomous, and strong; develop an independent legal and judicial system; undertake a radical transformation of its educational system; and fully reintegrate itself into the international economy. These reforms will also contribute greatly to the creation of a more just society. Greater efficiency and effectiveness in the government's social expenditures and higher average real wages resulting from the process of accelerated investment and economic growth will socially and politically strengthen the foundations of the new economic regime. I have sketched in broad strokes the path that must be taken in the process of transformation that is already under way. If Argentina follows this path, it will be in a good position to take off along a path of accelerated economic growth and convergence that will allow it, in the span of a generation, to rejoin the group of the most economically advanced nations to which it belonged in the 1920s and 1930s.

The lacerating civil war that began at the end of the 1960s, the painful defeat in the war for the Malvinas, the recurrent confiscations, the repudiation of the public debt, and the hyperinflationary convulsions that racked the country in 1989 and 1990 gave rise to a profound change in the attitudes of the majority of Argentines. Their isolationist and adversarial spirit in international matters, distrust of the workings of markets, and faith in state intervention have, in the face of ruinous failure, lost their force. Argentines have become more democratic in their political preferences and more privatist and pro-market in their economic preferences. They have finally accepted the advanced democratic nations as the model to emulate.

However, the road to success is riddled with potential pitfalls. There is always the possibility that external circumstances or damaging unexpected internal political events could lead Argentina into another economic crisis. There are also high social costs related to the transition (unemployment, plant closings, and bankruptcies) that spring from the contraction of the state's role and the profound restructuring of the private sector.

Finally, Argentina's future depends not only on the country's economic potential, but on the quality of its leadership, particularly on the leadership's perseverance in breaking with the past and completing the process of political and institutional reform begun with the return of democracy in 1983. Argentina's future will also depend on the ability of Argentine entrepeneurs, intellectuals, and politicians to create a radically different reality from the stifling and sad one that Argentina has known in recent decades.

In order to consolidate the important achievements that have been made so far, the next government, which will take office in July 1995, whatever its party affiliations, will have to make a determined effort to extend the reforms and, where necessary, correct the errors of implementation committed previously. Its ratification of ongoing economic reforms will probably be the decisive factor in bringing about the fall of long-term interest rates and completing a process of convergence between domestic interest rates and the interest rates of the most advanced countries. The disappearance of the country risk factor will then favor the start of a real boom of investment in productive activities. This will generate a virtuous circle in which high growth rates will promote large increases in the rates of savings and investment, which, in turn, will further accelerate the growth rate.

In the 1940s, Argentina was a rich country that assumed the vision and policies of a poor country, destroyed the fabric of its political system, and ended up transforming itself into an economically obsolete nation in a state of institutional decay. In 1994, Argentina is a straggler in the process of institutional modernization and a late bloomer in terms of economic development, but it has embarked on a process of profound political and economic reorganization which, if successfully completed during this decade, could pave the way for a vigorous economic recovery and economic convergence built on the solid foundation of a stable democratic political system.

APPENDIX

TABLE 1. ARGENTINA'S GROWTH RATES, AVERAGE
ANNUAL GDP AND PER CAPITA GDP

YEAR	POPULATION	RATES OF GDP GROWTH	PER CAPITA GDP
1900–05[a]	2.88	8.77	5.73
1906–10[a]	4.71	5.80	1.04
1911–13[a]	4.91	3.54	−1.31
1914–18[a]	2.20	−0.94	−3.07
1919–25[a]	4.00	7.98	3.83
1926–29[a]	2.85	5.67	2.74
1930–35[a]	2.39	0.33	−2.01
1936–40[a]	1.67	2.74	1.05
1941–45[a]	1.67	2.62	0.93
1946–50[a]	2.19	4.99	2.74
1946–50[b]			
1951–55[b]	1.99	2.98	0.97
1956–60[b]	1.72	2.97	1.22
1961–65[b]	1.57	4.38	2.77
1966–70[b]	1.46	4.27	2.76
1966–70[c]			
1971–75[c]	1.69	2.86	1.15
1976–80[c]	1.62	2.25	0.62
1976–80[d]			
1981–85[d]	1.60	−1.86	−3.41
1986–90[d]	1.47	0.03	−1.15

Source: Author's treatment on the basis of Banco Central de la República
Argentina, *Cuentas Nacionales, Series Históricas,* (1960, 1976, 1986),
and Comisión Económica para América Latina, *El desarrollo económico de la Argentina* (México City: CEPAL, 1959).
[a] 1950 prices, CEPAL.
[b] 1960 prices, BCRA.
[c] 1970 prices, BCRA.
[d] 1986 prices, BCRA − CEPAL.

TABLE 2. INVESTMENT AS A PERCENTAGE OF GDP FOR SELECTED COUNTRIES OR GROUPS OF COUNTRIES
(ANNUAL AVERAGE)

YEAR	ARGEN-TINA	BRAZIL	MEXICO	SPAIN	SOUTH KOREA	JAPAN	DEVELOPING COUNTRIES[a]	INDUSTRIAL-IZED COUNTRIES	WORLD AVERAGE
1960	21.8	18.7	16.7	19.0	10.9	32.6	19.0	23.3	22.2
1965	25.0	22.7	17.5	24.7	15.1	32.0	20.3	23.8	23.0
1970	22.2	25.5	22.7	24.5	25.4	39.1	22.3	24.4	24.2
1975	26.6	26.7	23.7	26.5	27.1	32.8	25.1	22.1	22.8
1980	26.6	22.5	28.1	21.2	31.1	32.3	26.1	23.5	24.1
1985	16.3	16.9	21.2	19.2	29.3	28.1	23.1	21.4	21.6
1986	17.5	19.1	18.5	20.0	28.3	27.7	22.5	21.1	21.4
1987	19.6	22.3	19.8	21.5	29.5	28.5	22.7	21.1	21.5
1988	19.5	22.8	20.4	23.8	30.6	30.4	23.3	21.6	21.9
1989	15.7	24.9	21.4	25.2	33.4	31.5	23.2	21.0	22.3
1990	14.2	21.7	21.9	25.8	36.9	32.6	23.4	21.4	22.3
1991	16.3		22.4	25.2	39.1	32.7		20.1	
1992	19.6				35.9	30.8		19.6	

Source: International Monetary Fund, *International Financial Statistics* (1960–1993).
[a] Non-oil exporting.

TABLE 3. ARGENTINA'S INVESTMENT/OUTPUT
AND CAPITAL/OUTPUT RATIOS

	INVESTMENT/ GDP %	CAPITAL/ GDP[a]	CAPITAL/ GDP[b]
1906–10		3.4	
1911–13	16.2	3.6	
1919–25	25.3	2.9	
1926–29	33.7	2.8	
1930–35	16.0	2.8	
1936–40	23.6	2.6	
1941–45	17.8	2.8	
1946–50	25.2	2.3	
1951–55	16.8	2.2	
1956–60	17.1	2.2	
1961–65	19.8	2.1	
1966–70	19.9	2.2	3.7
1971–75	21.9	2.5	3.9
1976–80	23.2	2.7	4.2
1981–85	19.7	3.4	5.2
1986–90	17.3	3.4	5.3

Source: Banco Central de la República Argentina, *Cuentas Nacionales de la República Argentina*. Series Históricas (1976); IEERAL, *Estadísticas de la Evolución de la Economía Argentina 1913–1984*, (1986). Samuel Goldberg, *Stock de Capital y Productividad* (Secretaria de Planificación, September 1991).
[a] For the last year of the period in question; after 1970 capital excludes housing investment.
[b] Includes housing investment.

TABLE 4. INDUSTRIAL PRODUCTION, WAGES, UNEMPLOYMENT AND ECONOMIC ACTIVITY IN ARGENTINA
(BASE 1986 = 100)

PERIOD	INDUSTRIAL PRODUCTION INDEX[a]	WAGES IN DOLLARS[b]	PURCHASING POWER OF WAGES INDEX[c]	UNEMPLOYMENT[d]	ECONOMICALLY ACTIVE POPULATION[e]
1980	98.2	—	90.3	—	—
1981	81.0	—	84.5	5.3%	38.3%
1982	83.9	—	74.3	4.6%	38.5%
1983	92.3	—	88.2	3.9%	37.3%
1984	96.7	291.7	104.3	4.4%	37.9%
1985	87.0	244.9	94.7	5.9%	38.2%
1986	100.0	306.8	100.0	5.2%	38.7%
1987	103.3	247.5	91.8	5.7%	38.9%
1988	98.3	251.6	81.8	6.1%	39.4%
1989	90.9	170.9	65.3	7.1%	39.3%
1990	89.0	373.3	70.5	6.3%	39.0%
Mar.1991	80.3	493.0	68.9	—	—

Jun.	88.7	519.2	75.9	6.9%	39.5%
Sep.	98.1	541.1	73.7	—	—
Dec.	96.6	563.1	74.0	6.0%	39.5%
Mar.1992	104.4	600.3	71.1	—	—
Jun.	104.1	634.7	72.3	6.9%	39.8%
Sep.	103.1	655.9	72.2	—	—
Dec.	97.8	663.0	72.3	7.0%	40.2%
Mar.1993	107.5	663.2	71.8	—	—
Jun.	106.1	675.3	70.9	9.9%	41.5%
Sep.	104.2	686.2	71.2	—	—
Dec.	106.5	693.4	71.3	9.3%	41.0%
Mar.1994	111.3	695.0	72.3	—	—
Jun.	110.8	698.4	72.8	10.8%	43.4%

[a]Seasonally adjusted. *Source*: FIEL.
[b]In dollars, at free exchange rates. *Source*: Carta Económica (1984–1994).
[c]*Source*: Author's treatment on the basis of FIEL data, *Indicadores de Coyuntura* (1980–1994).
[d/e]*Source*: INDEC. Data are for October for each year except 1994 when the data is for May (1980–1994).

TABLE 5. BREAKDOWN OF ARGENTINA'S TERMS OF TRADE
(BASED 1986 = 100)

YEAR	EXPORT PRICE INDEX	IMPORT PRICE INDEX	TERMS OF TRADE
1970	51.86	41.81	1.24
1975	107.74	90.33	1.19
1980	156.32	107.70	1.45
1981	163.20	104.20	1.57
1982	132.72	102.16	1.30
1983	120.16	95.16	1.26
1984	125.98	96.71	1.30
1985	113.80	96.33	1.18
1986	100.00	100.00	1.00
1987	96.19	111.53	0.86
1988	112.44	119.74	0.94
1989	120.53	129.56	0.93
1990	118.34	132.36	0.89
1991[a]	122.24	133.66	0.91
1992[a]	125.53	134.09	0.94
1993[a]	129.80	132.08	0.98

Source: Author's treatment based on Banco Central de la República Argentina, *Indicadores Económicos* (1970–1993).
[a] Preliminary figures.

TABLE 6. BREAKDOWN OF STOCK OF TOTAL FOREIGN DEBT BY CREDITOR (IN MILLIONS OF DOLLARS)

YEAR	BANKS	INTERNATIONAL AGENCIES	HOLDERS OF SECURITIES	PARIS CLUB	SUPPLIERS AND OTHERS	TOTAL
1983	31867	2893	4208		6101	45069
1984	32740	2818	4307		6306	46171
1985	33777	4569	3922	2061	4997	49326
1986	33695	5605	3638	4538	3946	51422
1987	36848	8320	3528	5302	4326	58324
1988	37277	8448	2915	5228	4605	58473
1989	38339	8160	5894	6090	4831	63314
1990	34979	9024	5668	6650	4652	60973
1991	30584	7704	5270[a]	8816	3623	55997[a]
1992	29311	7538	6845[a]	8835	6076	58605[a]
1993						64200[b]

Source: Author's treatment based on Banco Central de la Republica Argentina and Ministry of Economy data.
[a] Excludes BOCON (Debt Consolidation Bonds) issued in dollars.
[b] Author's estimate.

TABLE 7. EVOLUTION OF COUNTRY RISK PREMIUM
(PERCENTAGES)

COUNTRY PERIOD	BONEX YTM (REAL INTEREST RATE) (1)	6-MONTH LIBOR RATE (2)	COUNTRY RISK-FACTOR (1-2)
1981	16.2	16.7	(0.5)
1982	16.6	13.6	3.0
1983	18.1	9.9	8.2
1984	22.2	11.3	10.9
1985	18.9	8.6	10.3
1986	15.8	6.9	8.9
1987	18.3	7.3	11.0
1988	23.4	8.1	15.3
1989	28.7	9.3	19.4
1990	29.4	8.4	21.0
Mar. 1991	19.4	6.3	13.1
Jun.	17.9	6.6	11.3
Sep.	11.9	5.6	6.3
Dec.	11.0	4.3	6.7
Mar. 1992	10.8	4.6	6.2
Jun.	9.9	4.1	5.8
Sep.	10.5	3.4	7.1
Dec.	12.6	3.6	9.0
Mar. 1993	9.6	3.6	6.0
Jun.	7.2	3.5	3.7
Sep.	7.0	3.4	3.6
Dec.	7.0	3.4	3.6
Mar. 1994	10.3	4.1	6.2
Jun.	11.3	5.3	6.0
Sept.	10.4	5.7	4.7

Source: Author's treatment.
For the 1980–1990 period, the YTM (yield to maturity) for BONEX includes
    averages for each statistical series; for 1991–1993 the 1989 BONEX
    YTM was used.

TABLE 8. BREAKDOWN OF ARGENTINA'S AVERAGE REAL EXCHANGE RATES (BASE YEAR 1986 = 100)

PERIOD	DOLLARS[a]	CURRENCY BASKET[b]	EFFECTIVE REAL RATE, INDUSTRY[c]	EFFECTIVE REAL RATE, IMPORTS[d]
1980	39.5	46.2	51.6	
1981	47.9	51.8	63.3	
1982	82.4	83.9	98.5	
1983	97.4	93.6	113.4	
1984	90.8	80.7	102.2	
1985	105.7	89.4	107.5	
1986	100	100	100	100
1987	103	110.6	108.2	101.6
1988	98.3	109.5	104.9	101.4
1989	133.1	146.6	118.9	120.5
First Qtr.'90	119.7	146.3	112.8	103.8
Second Qtr.'90	100.9	111.3	85.4	78.3
Third Qtr.'90	79.7	96.5	80.4	66.1
Fourth Qtr.'90	60.3	74.4	62.5	50.8
First Qtr.'91	68.3	80.4	68.6	58.1
Second Qtr.'91	68	79.5	65.4	51.3
Third Qtr.'91	66.5	78.5	63.5	49.8
Fourth Qtr.'91	65.6	79.2	62.6	49.2

(*continued*)

TABLE 8. BREAKDOWN OF ARGENTINA'S AVERAGE REAL EXCHANGE RATES (BASE YEAR 1986 = 100)
(continued)

PERIOD	DOLLARS[a]	CURRENCY BASKET[b]	EFFECTIVE REAL RATE, INDUSTRY[c]	EFFECTIVE REAL RATE, IMPORTS[d]
First Qtr.'92	64	77.8	61.3	47.8
Second Qtr.'92	62.9	76.5	60.3	46.7
Third Qtr.'92	61.6	77.8	59.2	45.9
Fourth Qtr.'92	61.5	74.7	60.8	47.0
First Qtr.'93	61.3	72.7	62.0	
Second Qtr.'93	60.4	72.5		
Third Qtr.'93	60.1	71.1		
Fourth Qtr.'93	60.2	70.7		
First Qtr.'94	60.4	70.9		
Second Qtr.'94	60.2	72.3		

Source: Banco Central de la República Argentina, Indicadores Económicos (1980–1993), and author's estimates.
[a] Average sellers' exchange rate deflated by average Consumer Price Index and National Wholesale Non-Agricultural Prices, and the U.S. Consumer Price Index.
[b] Same as [a], divided by a basket of currencies weighted for their average participation in 1992 foreign trade.
[c] Average exchange rate adjusted for drawbacks and tax credits, and weighted by the value of exports for 1988.
[d] Average exchange rate adjusted for import duties and weighted by the value of imports for 1988.

TABLE 9. EVOLUTION OF RELATIVE PRICES IN ARGENTINA
(COMPARATIVE CONSUMER PRICE INDEX LEVELS; BASE YEAR 1988 = 100)

Period	Total	Food Goods	Industrial Goods	Total	Private Services	Public Services
1980	98.1	92.1	105.1	103.7	118.8	75.6
1981	95.3	89.5	102.1	109.2	119.7	89.6
1982	103.6	96.1	111.2	93.0	99.8	80.3
1983	105.8	96.1	116.9	88.6	90.6	84.9
1984	104.6	96.2	114.3	90.9	95.4	82.7
1985	98.6	90.9	107.5	102.8	108.8	91.6
1986	97.2	96.7	97.7	105.6	116.8	84.7
1987	96.2	97.6	94.7	107.4	119.7	84.4
1988	99.7	98.5	101.2	100.5	103.1	95.8
1989	107.5	100.6	115.6	85.2	91.9	72.5
1990	84.9	86.3	104.9	110.0	129.7	72.2
Mar.1991	86.3	74.5	99.8	127.0	153.8	71.8

(continued)

TABLE 9. EVOLUTION OF RELATIVE PRICES IN ARGENTINA
(COMPARATIVE CONSUMER PRICE INDEX LEVELS; BASE YEAR 1988 = 100) (continued)

Period	Total	Food Goods	Industrial Goods	Total	Private Services	Public Services
Jun.	85.4	78.3	93.3	128.7	157.9	68.6
Sep.	84.9	78.5	91.8	129.9	161.4	64.8
Dec.	83.4	79.0	89.5	132.7	166.6	63.0
Mar.1992	82.8	81.5	84.3	133.9	168.4	62.6
Jun.	81.5	80.9	82.3	136.5	172.2	63.1
Sep.	80.7	78.6	81.7	138.0	174.6	62.6
Dec.	79.6	80.1	140.3			
Mar.1993	79.1	79.6	78.2	141.2		
Jun.	79.1	82.9	76.4	141.1		

Source: Banco Central de la República Argentina, *Indicadores Económicos* (1980–1994).

TABLE 10. BREAKDOWN OF ARGENTINA'S PRINCIPAL
MONETARY AGGREGATES, MONTHLY AVERAGE FOR DAILY
BALANCES (IN MILLIONS OF DOLLARS)

	MONETARY BASE	M1	M3	ADJUSTED M3[a]
Jun. 1989	1,297	1,217	5,325	5,897
Dec.	1,575	1,613	3,872	5,515
Jun. 1990	3,012	2,951	4,953	6,334
Dec.	6,955	5,600	11,222	14,064
Mar. 1991	4,317	3,575	7,270	9,127
Jun.	5,581	5,291	9,316	11,868
Sep.	6,214	6,088	10,549	15,039
Dec.	7,608	7,860	12,844	19,404
Mar. 1992	8,495	8,533	14,363	22,262
Jun.	9,826	9,830	17,363	26,420
Sep.	10,232	10,457	19,124	29,467
Dec.	11,018	11,561	20,299	31,225
Mar. 1993	10,652	11,901	22,704	35,700
Jun.	12,146	13,051	24,797	38,850
Sep.	14,789	14,216	27,424	43,992
Dec.	15,001	15,322	29,073	47,176
Mar. 1994	15,081	17,073	32,336	51,986
Jun.	15,403	16,666	32,380	53,302
Sept.	15,615	16,840	32,620	54,600

Source: Author's treatment on Banco Central de la República Argentina,
Boletín Estadístico (1989–1994).
[a]Includes M3 plus foreign currency deposits in the domestic banking system.

GLOSSARY

BCRA:	Banco Central de la República Argentina
CARI:	Consejo Argentino para las Relaciones Internacionales
CEDES:	Centro de Estudios de Estado y Sociedad
CEPAL:	Comisión Económica para América Latina
EUDEBA:	Editorial de la Universidad de Buenos Aires
FIEL:	Fundación de Investigaciones Económicas Latinoamericanas
IEERAL:	Instituto de Estudios Económicos sobre la Realidad Argentina y Latinoamericana
NBER:	National Bureau of Economic Research
OEA:	Organización de Estados Americanos
OECD:	Organization for Economic Cooperation and Development

NOTES

CHAPTER 1

1. See Colin Clark, *The Conditions of Economic Progress* (London: Macmillan, 1951); Simon Kuznets, *Economic Growth and Structure: Selected Essays* (London: Heinemann, 1965); Joseph Schumpeter, *Capitalism, Socialism and Democracy* (New York: Harper, 1942); and David Landes, *The Unbound Prometheus: Technological Change and Industrial Development in Western Europe from 1750 to the Present* (Cambridge: Cambridge University Press, 1965).
2. See Jacob Schmookler, *Invention and Economic Growth* (Cambridge: Harvard University Press, 1966); Edwin Mansfield, "How Rapidly Does New Industrial Technology Leak Out?" *Journal of Industrial Economics*, no. 91 (1985), pp. 907–18; and Patrice Higonnet, David Landes, and Henry Rosovsky, *Favorites of Fortune: Technology, Growth, and Economic Development Since the Industrial Revolution* (Cambridge: Harvard University Press, 1991).
3. See Gene Grossman and Elhanan Helpman, *Innovation and Growth in the Global Economy* (Cambridge: MIT Press, 1991).
4. See Edward F. Denison, *Trends in American Economic Growth, 1929–1982* (Washington, D.C.: Brookings Institution, 1985); William Baumol, "Productivity, Growth, Convergence and Welfare: What the Long-Run Data Show," *American Economic Review* 76 (December 1986), pp. 1072–85; and J. Bradford De Long, "Productivity Growth, Convergence and Welfare: Comment," *American Economic Review* 78 (December 1988), pp. 1138–54.
5. See J. Bradford De Long and Lawrence Summers, "Equipment Investment and Economic Growth," *Quarterly Journal of Economics* 106 (May 1991), pp. 445–502.

6. For discussions of the importance of human capital in generating and disseminating technological innovation, see Paul Romer, "Increasing Returns and Long-Run Growth," *Journal of Political Economy* 94 (1986), pp. 1002–37; and Robert Lucas, "On the Mechanics of Economic Development," *Journal of Monetary Economics* 22 (1988), pp. 3–42.

7. See Robert Barro, "Economic Growth in a Cross-Section of Countries," *Quarterly Journal of Economics* 106 (May 1991), pp. 407–43.

8. See Angus Maddison, *Phases of Capitalist Development* (Oxford: Oxford University Press, 1982); ibid., "A Comparison of Levels of GDP Per Capita in Developed and Developing Countries, 1700–1980," *Journal of Economic History* 43 (March 1983), pp. 27–41; ibid., "Growth and Slowdown in Advanced Capitalist Economies: Techniques of Quantitative Assessment," *Journal of Economics* 25 (June 1987), pp.669–738; Baumol, "Productivity, Growth, Convergence and Welfare;" and Robert Barro, "Government Spending in a Simple Model of Endogenous Growth," *Journal of Political Economy* 98 (1990), pp. 5103–25.

9. Economists usually distinguish between production efficiency (internal efficiency, or X) and efficiency of resource allocation (exchange efficiency, or A). Production efficiency, or firm efficiency, is that which allows an increase in the quantity or quality of a product or service without increased use of production factors. Even if an activity is productively efficient, the price environment, market characteristics, or regulations can lead to the selection of inappropriate production techniques or locations and/or to rationing of supply and demand below optimum levels (inefficient resource allocation).

10. Kuznets, *Economic Growth and Structure*.

11. Clark, *Conditions of Economic Progress*.

12. See Thorstein Veblen, *Imperial Germany and the Industrial Revolution* (London: Macmillan, 1915); Maddison, *Phases of Capitalist Development*; Arthur Lewis, *Growth and Fluctuations, 1870–1913* (London: Allen and Unwin, 1978); and Cynthia Morris and Irma Adelman, *Comparative Patterns of Economic Growth* (Baltimore: Johns Hopkins University Press, 1988).

13. See Arthur Lewis, *The Theory of Economic Growth* (London: Allen and Unwin, 1955).

14. *El desarrollo económico de la Argentina* (Mexico City: CEPAL, 1959).

15. *The Economist Book of Vital World Statistics*, (New York: Random House, 1990).

CHAPTER 2

1. See Paul Bairoch, "Écarts internationaux des niveaux de vie avant la revolution industrielle," *Annales, économies, sociétés, civilisations*, no. 34 (January 1979), pp. 145–71.
2. Maddison, *Phases of Capitalist Development*.
3. CEPAL, *El desarrollo económico de la Argentina;* Carlos Díaz Alejandro, *Essays on the Economic History of the Argentine Republic* (New Haven: Yale University Press, 1970); and sources indicated for table 3 and graph 1.
4. See Guido Di Tella and Manuel Zymelman, *Las etapas del desarrollo económico argentino* (Buenos Aires: EUDEBA, 1967).
5. CEPAL, *El desarrollo económico de la Argentina*.
6. Di Tella and Zymelman, *Las etapas del desarrollo económico argentino*.
7. V. L. Phelps, *The International Economic Position of Argentina* (New York: University of Pennsylvania Press, 1938).
8. Roger Gravil, *The Anglo-Argentine Connection, 1900–1939*, Dellplain Latin America Studies, no. 16 (Boulder, Col.: Westview Press, 1985).
9. *Education, Human Resources and Development in Argentina* (Paris: OECD, 1967).
10. Díaz Alejandro, *Essays on the Economic History of the Argentine Republic*.
11. Díaz Alejandro, *Essays on the Economic History of the Argentine Republic*; and IEERAL, *Estudios: Estadísticas de la evolución económica de Argentina, 1913–1984* (Cordoba: July–September 1986).
12. CEPAL, *El desarrollo económico de la Argentina*.
13. IEERAL, *Estudios: Estadísticas de las evolución económica de Argentina*.
14. CEPAL, *El desarrollo económico de la Argentina*; A. Porto, "Una revisión crítica de las empresas publicas en argentina," in Pablo Gerchunoff, ed., *Las privatizaciones en la Argentina* (Buenos Aires: Instituto Torcuato di Tella, 1992), pp. 165–213.
15. See Alexander Gerschenkron, *Economic Backwardness in Historical Perspective* (Cambridge: Harvard University Press, 1962); Moses Abramovitz, *Thinking About Growth* (New York: Cambridge University Press, 1989); and Baumol, "Productivity, Growth, Convergence, and Welfare."
16. Mancur Olson, *The Rise and Decline of Nations* (New Haven: Yale University Press, 1982).
17. See Anne Krueger, "The Political Economy of the 'Rent-Seeking' Society," *American Economic Review* 64 (1974), pp. 291–303.

18. Vitorio Corbo, Anne Krueger, and F. Ossa, eds., *Export Oriented Development Strategies* (Boulder, Col.: Westview Press, 1985); Adolfo C. Sturzenegger, *Comercio exterior, Crecimiento Económico y Política Comercial: Interrelaciones, Efectos y Esquemas Alternativos para Argentina* (Buenos Aires: Asociación de Bancos Argentinos, 1986); Felipe A. M. de la Balze (ed.), *El Comercio Exterior Argentina en la Década de 1990* (Buenos Aires: CARI/Manantial, 1991).

19. Díaz Alejandro, *Essays on the Economic History of the Argentine Republic.*

20. Di Tella and Zymelman, *Las etapas del desarrollo económico argentino.*

21. See CEPAL, *El desarrollo económico de la Argentina*; Rogelio Frigerio, *Nacionalismo, potencias industriales y subdesarrollo* (Buenos Aires: Editorial Concordia, 1961); and Raúl Prebisch, *Problemas teóricos y practicos del crecimiento económico* (New York: Naciones Unidas, EICON12, 1952).

22. See Díaz Alejandro, *Essays on the Economic History of the Argentine Republic*; Domingo Cavallo and Joaquin Cottani, *The Timing and Sequence of Trade Liberalization Policies: The Case of Argentina* (Washington, D.C.: World Bank, 1986); and Adolfo C. Sturzenegger, *Mercado, Plan, Crecimiento, Estabilidad en Argentina*, Ensayos Económicos, no. 31 (Banco Central de la República Argentina, September 1984), pp. 67–91; and ibid., "Apertura de la economía," *Estudios*, no. 57 (Enero/ Marzo 1991), pp. 33–43.

23. See Jorge Katz and Bernardo Kosacoff, *El sector manufacturero argentino: maduración, retroceso y prospectiva* (Buenos Aires: CEPAL, 1988); and Alfred Chandler, *"Scale and Scope": The Dynamics of Industrial Enterprise* (Cambridge: Harvard University Press, 1990).

24. See Y. Mundlak, D. Cavallo, and R. Domenech, *Agriculture and Economic Growth in Argentina, 1913–1984*, Research Report No. 76 (Washington, D.C.: International Food Policy Research Institute, 1986).

25. See Marcelo Diamand, *Doctrinas económicas e independencia* (Buenos Aires: Paidos, 1973); and Aldo Ferrer, *Crisis y alternativas de la política económica argentina* (Mexico: Fondo de Cultura Economica, 1979).

26. Neostructuralist economic policies can work in mixed economies under certain institutional conditions, as in the cases of Japan and South Korea. On the former, see William Lockwood, *The Economic Development of Japan: Growth and Structural Change, 1868–1938* (Princeton: Princeton University Press, 1954), and Toru Yanagihara, *The Asia Pacific Economic Zone and the Role*

of Japan (Tokyo: Hosei University, 1992); on the latter, see Alice Amsden, *Asia's Next Giant: South Korea and Late Industrialization* (Oxford: Oxford University Press, 1989).

27. See Olson, *Rise and Decline of Nations*; and Amsden, *Asia's Next Giant*.

28. Jean Claude García Zamor, *Public Administration and Social Changes in Argentina* (Rio de Janeiro: Casa Vallelle, 1968).

29. See OEA, *Estudios sobre la administración pública en America Latina: Argentina* (Washington, D.C.: 1968).

30. Kathryn Sikkink, "Las capacidades y la autonomia del estado en Brasil y las Argentina; Un enfoque neo-institucionalista," *Desarrollo Económico*, no. 128 (January–March 1993), pp. 8502–541.

31. Peter Smith, *Labyrinths of Power: Political Recruitment in Twentieth-Century Mexico* (Princeton: Princeton University Press, 1979).

32. Luis Beccaria, "Distribución del ingreso en la Argentina: explorando lo sucedido desde mediados de los setenta," *Desarrollo Económico*, no.123 (October–December 1991), 321–38.

33. José M. Fanelli and Roberto Frenkel, *On Gradualism, Shock and Sequencing in Economic Adjustment*, Document No. 87 (Buenos Aires: CEDES, July 1992).

34. Felipe A. M. de la Balze, ed., *El financiamento externo argentino durante la década de 1990* (Buenos Aires: CARI/Sudamericana, 1989).

35. Silvio Borner, Aymo Brunetti, and Beatrice Weder, *Institutional Obstacles to Latin American Growth* (San Francisco: International Center for Economic Growth, 1992).

36. Jorge Avila has demonstrated the high correlation (in a medium-sized economy open to the world such as Argentina's) between fiscal and "quasi-fiscal" lack of control and high uncertainty and volatility for key prices (salaries, exchange rates, and interest rates measured in real terms). On the basis of a statistical comparison with other countries, Avila noticed a clear negative correlation between, on the one hand, fiscal deficit and volatility in relative prices and, on the other hand, investment levels and rates of economic growth. *El valor económico de la certidumbre*, Ensayos Económicos No. 41 (Banco Central de la Republica Argentina, July 1989), pp. 1–25.

37. Díaz Alejandro, *Essays on the Economic History of the Argentine Republic*; Cavallo and Cottani, *Timing and Sequence of Trade Liberalization Policies*.

38. Julio Nogues, *Políticas de promoción de exportaciones y aplicación de derechos compensatorios*, Ensayos Económicos No. 41

(Banco Central de la Republica Argentina, July 1989), pp. 33–52.

39. Bernardo Kosacoff and Daniel Aspiazu, *La industria Argentina: desarrollo y cambios estructurales* (Buenos Aires: Centro Editor de America Latina, 1989).

40. *The Economist Book of Vital World Statistics*, 1990, pp. 42, 48, 204–5.

41. Ibid., pp. 154–55.

42. The most important empirical study done in Argentina about sources of economic growth confirms the conclusions reached in this chapter. Following Edward F. Denison's methodology, Victor Elias examined data regarding Argentina's economic growth between 1940 and 1980. These data confirm the sharp drop in the efficiency and productivity of the Argentine economy. The contribution of factors not related to quantity and quality of labor and capital (among others, market size, economic organization, and technology assimilation) fell from 60 percent in the 1940s, to 25 percent in the 1950s, to 5 percent in the 1960s, and became negative in the 1970s. The data also confirm the major increases in investment levels from 1960 to 1980 and the low efficiency and productivity of such investments (*Sources of Growth: A Study of Seven Latin American Economies* [San Francisco: International Center for Economic Growth, 1992]).

CHAPTER 3

1. I refer here to income policies that tried to fix relative prices in order to improve fiscal revenue by fixing and subsequently freezing public-sector wages and rates, price controls, devaluation followed by the fixing of exchange rates, and the implementation of mechanisms to discourage speculation in order to control expectations and eliminate the "inflationary inertia."

2. See M. Bruno, ed., *Inflación y estabilización: La experiencia de Israel, Argentina, Brasil, Bolivia y México* (Mexico City: Fondo de Cultura Económica, 1988); and Adolfo Canitrot, "Programas de ajuste y estrategias políticas," *Desarrollo Económico*, no. 121 (April–June 1991), pp. 125–33.

3. A measure of the distribution of tariffs in terms of the average tariff. The tariffs dispersion is usually measured as the average tariff, plus or minus the average deviation among tariffs in effect and their average value.

4. The sum of all factors that contribute to the ability and willingness of debtors within a country to respond to their foreign obligations within the established payment periods.

5. Felipe A. M. de la Balze (ed.), *El financiamiento externo argentino durante la década de 1990* (Buenos Aires: CARI/Sudamericana, 1989).
6. Porto, "Una revisión critica de las empresas publicas."
7. See Pablo Gerchunoff and Alieto Guadagni, *Elementos para un programa de reformulación económica del Estado* (Buenos Aires: Instituto Torcuato di Tella, 1987).
8. FIEL, *El Fracaso del Estatismo* (Buenos Aires: Sudamericana-Planeta, 1987); and *Capital de infrastructura en la Argentina: gestión pública, privatización y productividad* (Buenos Aires: FIEL, 1992).
9. Felipe A. M. de la Balze (ed.), *El financiamiento externo argentino*.
10. FIEL, *Capital de infrastructura en la Argentina*.
11. Pablo Rojo, "Desregulación de la económia argentina," *Novedades Económicas*, no. 39 (August 1992), pp. 123–32.
12. FIEL, *La reforma económica, 1989–1991: Balance y perspectivas* (Buenos Aires: Manantial, 1991).
13. Oscar D. Cetrangolo and José L. Machinea, *El Sistema Previsional Argentino: Crisis y Transición*, Documento de trabajo No. 6 (Buenos Aires: Instituto para el Desarrollo Industrial, January 1993).
14. Ibid.
15. It is important to note that preferential tariffs granted in the framework of MERCORUS do not apply to the statistical fee, for which reason such a mechanism has a direct impact on intraregional levels of protection.
16. The measure of protection that allows for a restriction on imports, calculated as a percentage of value added for the product in question.
17. Julio Nogues, "Observaciones sobre los vínculos existentes entre los subsidios y la decadercia económica de la Argentina," *Desarrollo Económico*, no. 117 (April–June 1990), pp. 85–107.
18. The quotient between the effective rate of exchange for exports and the effective rate of exchange for imports, adjusted for the effect of quotas.

CHAPTER 4

1. See Amsden, *Asia's Next Giant*; Lockwood, *Economic Development of Japan*; and Veblen, *Imperial Germany*.
2. To "hoard" is to increase liquid assets with no specific aim, typically as a "hedge" or as a kind of precautionary measure.
3. Amsden, *Asia's Next Giant*.

4. CEPAL, *El desarrollo económico de la Argentina*.
5. See Peter Evans, Dietrich Rueschemeyer, and Theda Skocpol, *Bringing the State Back In* (Cambridge: Cambridge University Press, 1985); David Landau, "Government Expenditure and Economic Growth: A Cross-Country Study," *Southern Economic Journal*, no. 49 (1983), pp. 783–92; and Jorge Roulet and Jorge Sabato, *Estado y administración publica en la Argentina*, Polemica No. 78 (Buenos Aires: Centro Editor de America Latina, 1971).
6. See, for example, Paul Romer, "Human Capital and Growth: Theory and Evidence," NBER Working Paper No. 3173 (Cambridge, Mass., 1989); and Barro, "Economic Growth in a Cross Section of Countries."
7. See *Decentralización de la escuela primaria y media* (Buenos Aires: FIEL, 1993); and José Luis de Imaz, *Informe blanco sobre el sistema educativo argentino* (Buenos Aires: Fundación Banco de Boston, 1993).
8. See Michael Porter, *The Competitive Advantage of Nations* (Free Press, 1990).
9. See Porter, *Competitive Advantage*; and Lester Thurow, *Head to Head* (New York: Morrow, 1992).
10. Marcelo Castro Corbat, ed., *Informe 84* (Buenos Aires: Talleres Thonegger, 1984).

INDEX

ABOUT THE AUTHOR

Felipe A.M. de la Balze, businessman, investment banker, and academic, has written several books on Argentina's reform, including *Reforma y Convergencia* (CARI, 1993), *El Comercio Exterior Argentino durante la Década de 1990* (CARI, 1991), and *El Financiamiento Externo Argentino durante la Década de 1990* (CARI, 1989). He is a professor of international economics at the Foreign Affairs and National Defense Schools, a member of the Executive Committee of the Consejo Argentino de Relaciones Internacionales (CARI) and sits on the board of several Argentine companies including Banco República, Siderar, and Citicorp Equity Investments. He studied at the Institut d'Etudes Politiques (Paris University), the Woodrow Wilson School (Princeton University) and the London School of Economics.